LIVING *in the* IN-BETWEEN TIMES

The Life of Samuel

RALPH DOUGLAS WEST

LIVING *in the* IN-BETWEEN TIMES

The Life of Samuel

HUPOMONE PRESS
FORT WORTH, TEXAS

Library of Congress Cataloging-in-Publication Data
Living in the In-between Times/
Ralph D. West, Sr., author, 1959-
ISBN: 978-1-4675-2794-1900-0

DEDICATION

A. LOUIS PATTERSON, JR.

MOUNT CORINTH MISSIONARY BAPTIST CHURCH
HOUSTON, TEXAS

Pastor, Mentor, Friend

Excellent in exposition, unexcelled in insight,
unequalled in creativity
Pastor of pastors, preacher to the nations, prophet
for the world

CONTENTS

FOREWORD

Open your Bible and your life and follow Dr. Ralph Douglas West, Sr. as he takes you on a journey into the lives of ancient heroes, triumphant and tragic, and brings them into your life. The author explores episodes in the lives of Hannah, Samuel, Saul, and others, hearing God's voice and gleaning His truth. Showing a keen insight into the dynamic of the Holy Scriptures, this book allows you to hear what they heard (and even what they missed).

I listen regularly to sermons by Dr. West, either on the broadcasts of his worship services on cable television or podcasts online, and I am often drawn into biblical scenes through his preaching. These written accounts show his adeptness in making biblical scenes and characters vivid. His extraordinary gift of storytelling makes this book a very enjoyable read. You will not want to put it down.

More importantly, this book is written by one who has walked with God and lived in and out of the Word of God daily, season after season. So, in the narrative God speaks, and His truth is revealed in the normal flow of the stories. Reading each episode gives you a great opportunity to sit with someone who knows God and this world of the Bible very well.

As one who teaches the Old Testament to seminary students, I can see the evidence of Dr. West's extensive research behind this book. Yet, the scholarly insights inform his interpretation of these episodes without unduly intruding into the narrative. This is a masterful work, and a great example for young scholarly preachers and ministers who have a calling to serve the church.

Because I am a preacher, I find the use of stories and illustrations in this book very helpful in understanding and applying the truths of these Scriptures to my life. Yet, they are also used artistically to enhance what the text is saying without getting in the way. The illustrations are also used as bridges into life, which shows the work of a skillful preacher.

Now, read and be blessed. I was.

—*Ronald L. Cook*
Director, Doctor of Ministry Program
Associate Professor of Christian Scriptures
George W. Truett Theological Seminary
Baylor University
Waco, Texas

PREFACE

At every level of human experience you may find yourself "in between the times." The second hand on your old watch pauses slightly in between the seconds. Your heart pauses momentarily between beats. The music stops for a second when the score indicates a rest. The team sits in the locker room at the half. The pitcher glances at third before he throws. The conductor holds his baton in the air before it falls. The sprinter takes his stance and looks at the ground before the starter's gun sounds. They are all "in between the times."

Sometimes those "living in between the times" intervals last longer. A baby is conceived, and the expected nine months are "in between the times." An engagement ring is offered and accepted, and then the couple is living "in between the times." The doctor gives a diagnosis that changes everything. The patient takes a round of treatments, waiting to see if the prescription works and health returns. The acceptance letter comes from the university in the spring, but the freshman year does not begin until fall. The Human Resources department offers the job, but it does not begin for three months. The orderlies roll your beloved into the operating room, but the doctor does not come out for four hours.

How much of your life do you spend "in between the times"? Waiting in lines, sitting at the end of the runway waiting for the take-off, waiting to go to sleep, staring at the phone and praying it will ring . . . . all of these activities mark that margin called "in between the times." In one way or another, all of us are living in that no man's land all of the time. In fact, living between the times just belongs to the human condition.

The planet itself lives in between the times. The world right now exists in an in-between time known as an interglacial time. The last ice age was about 11,000 years ago. Yet you did not wake up this morning and say to your spouse, "Honey, remember we are in between the ice ages." Nevertheless, the world does spin its way around the sun in between the glacial times. (By the way, you really do not have to worry about the next ice age because it will probably reach its peak in about 80,000 years. That is a long in-between time.)

History also reveals in-between times. After the death of Alexander the Great, the western world was divided into areas dominated by his generals. The next historical strongman, Julius Caesar, did not show up until 223 years after Alexander's death. The West lived for centuries in that in-between time, awaiting the next gigantic figure. After the fall of the Roman Empire in A.D. 476, the West lived for centuries in another in-between time called the Dark Ages. After the Enlightenment era in the 18th century, people lived in what some call the Modern Age, until the beginning of the Post-Modern Age in the 1960s. Yet, some pundits debate that we are still living in an in-between time today.

Wherever you touch life, whether it involves the individual, the planet, or history, you will find in-between times. Consider just one definition of time: "a nonspatial continuum in which events occur in apparently irreversible succession from the past through the present to the future." That very definition demonstrates how impossible it is to capture what now means. In fact, philosophers debate at length what the word *now* means. The very moment you have said *now*, it is no longer *now*, but *then*. The now in the future will immediately become *then*. In a way, we are always living in between the times.

Samuel belonged to the in-between times regarding God's dealings with His people and their destiny. Abraham walked with God almost a thousand years before Samuel. The Hebrews walked out of Egypt hundreds of years before Samuel. Joshua fought centuries before that. After the Hebrews settled the land God had promised them, they lived as a loosely associated group of kinfolks in twelve tribes. They had no king but

God. Yet, a disastrous cycle stamped their lives. God would deliver them with a charismatic judge, and they would thrive for a period of time. Then they would disobey, and God would use an external enemy to threaten them. Then God would raise up another judge to deliver them. These ups and downs marked the history of God's people immediately before Samuel came on the scene.

Samuel lived in an in-between time. He was both the last of the charismatic judges and the first of the prophets. Before him was chaos, but after him came kings. He stood on a border in time. On one side of the border were people who wanted God as their king, yet they failed Him. On the other side of the border were the three kings of the "United Hebrew Monarchy": Saul, David, and Solomon. After Solomon came the tragic civil war that ripped the nation into two nations—north and south—never to be reconciled again. In every sense Samuel lived in the in-between times.

Today, do we sense that we are living in between the times? The tragedy of 9/11 looms behind us as a bracket in time. An organized war on terror has defined a decade. With troops scheduled to return from Iraq and Afghanistan, the nation awaits another chapter—a new era. Complicating this has been the economic collapse of 2008 and the current recovery awaiting another time of relative prosperity. Such realities mark us as those who live in between the times.

When God's people live in a current reality that parallels the biblical reality, we need to find figures inhabiting the same world we inhabit. We can move in with them for a while and live beside them, watching them arrange the furniture of their times. We can read their mail over their shoulders. We can find the clues they left behind in the attics and desk drawers of their lives by sorting through their file folders or getting their user ID and password and reading their e-mail.

We may try that very thing with this man named Samuel. His name has been given to at least a million boys, past and present. Two books in the Old Testament carry his name. He lives closer to your address than you may think. You might just want to hang out with him for a while. He will not shout at you. You can hear him whisper over 3,000 years ago about living in the in-between times.

CHAPTER ONE

Samuel: An Overview

We have all known someone whose name does not match who they really are. A "Slim" who is anything but. A "Shorty" who is taller than six feet. A "Jim" whose actual name is not "James." And of course, a "Doc" who has never seen the inside of a college, much less a medical school. Such is the ironic nature of names.

Many biblical names hold up to closer examination. That may be true with our man in the middle, Samuel. Two translations of his Hebrew name carry weight. Some believe his name refers to his experience as a little boy who heard the voice of God (1 Samuel 1:29). For them his name should be translated, "God hears." Others consider that the Hebrew name bears the very name of God Himself, "Name of God." Either understanding gives you a clue not only to the name, but also to the nature of this person of God. He carried in his very name the mission of his life. You could not hear his name without thinking of the God he heard and served.

Now, most of us have a common name that does not have theological significance. Yet we can live in such a way that the very thought of us reminds people of the God we serve. Your name may be Tyrone, Ralph, Lateisha, Harry, or something else. You too can live in such a way that the very calling of your name reminds people of the Lord you serve. The very thought of your identity could point people to the Living One. What is the first thing that comes into someone's mind when they think of your identity?

Samuel is the man in the middle because he stands between one kind of charismatic leader called "judge" and the next type of anointed godly servant called "prophet." Zoom out on the story of God's people with me and get the big picture. About 4,000 years ago God called a man in what is today Iraq to leave everything he had and walk into the desert with Him. That man was Abram, and his wife was Sarah. Genesis 12 and following tells the story of that man and his family: Isaac, Jacob, and Joseph. When the Book of Exodus opens, the descendants of Abraham (his new name after God breathed on him) are living in slavery under the superpower of the times, Egypt. God appointed Moses to lead the Hebrews out of slavery, and then He delivered them with signs of His power. Because of their disobedience and doubt, they walked around in circles in the desert for 40 years.

When Moses died, his associate Joshua took over as

CEO of Exodus, Inc. and led the people into the land that God promised. Joshua was a warrior as well as governor. The Hebrews conquered much of the land, occupied the Vermont-sized conquest in tribal areas, and started a new life as a loose confederation of twelve tribes.

When you zoom out on holy history, you may be reminded that all of us have a history with God. Indeed, some of us have a long family history with Him; generations of our people have called on Him. Others of us only have our own history with God, but we *do* have a history.

To this point of the story, you will not observe any sinless saints, perfect followers, or easy path. That is the way of faith. You will also notice that God used an astounding set of imperfect characters. Abraham lied about his wife. Isaac appears as a weaker person than Abraham. Jacob is a scam artist. Joseph talks too much and gets into trouble with his brothers. Moses kills an Egyptian. Joshua is timid about following in the shadow of Moses. Sarah misses the will of God when she tells Abraham to sleep with her maid. Rebekah fools her own blind husband. Moses' sister misunderstands her brother's mission. A whore named Rahab helps Joshua take down a city.

What a cast of characters God uses for His purposes! Not one of them is perfect, but all are people of faith.

That cast gives me some hope. Maybe I can be in the family.

Towards the end of the period of the charismatic judges, Samuel emerged as a transitional leader, between the times. His parents Elkanah and Hannah lived in the hill country, elevated above flat plains beneath. Sometimes geography represents individual destiny. A case in point is this couple, who lived where they could see farther. Yet even though they expressed devotion to Israel's God, a shadow fell across their sunny hillside cottage. No child's voice filled their house. The days were quiet and peaceful, but the quietness was also one marked by absence.

The lack of a child in that culture moved Hannah to pray at the shrine where the remote figure Eli, considered the last of the judges, presided over the worship of God. As a response to her heartbreak, God gave a son to the couple—little Samuel. Hannah dedicated him to the Lord and kept her word. She sent him to boarding school at the shrine. There is always a note of pathos in the tender story when she wove him a robe and took it to him at the shrine. The little one God gave her she gave back to God.

The story of Hannah praying for a son at the shrine of Shiloh belongs to one of the most beloved chapters in the Bible. The old judge Eli thought she was drunk because she was praying with such intensity. He then found out that she was indeed very sober as she was begging God for a child. She promised to give that child back to God if He would just give her the child.

When you give back to God what He gives to you, the outcome is always better than you can imagine. The famed preacher James Earl Massey was a concert pianist when God called him to preach. He turned his back on his personal aspirations and gave his life to God for whatever purposes God wished to use him. Yet God gave him back both his original gifts and added to that the gift of a teacher of preachers. He continued both to play the piano in concerts and preach. Not long ago at Baylor University, he spoke to church musicians from all over the nation, using both his original gift and the additional calling that God had given him. Indeed, you can trust God when you give back to Him what He gave to you.

Surely one of the most beloved scenes in the Old Testament occurs when God speaks to the little boy Samuel to affirm him and ordain his vocation. When Samuel was about 13 years old, according to the rabbis, God spoke to him three times at the compound of Eli. The first and second times the elder Eli sent Samuel back to sleep. The third time the old judge recognized that it was the voice of God speaking to little Samuel.

Samuel received his vocation and stepped forward into immortality in the family of God.

Surely the very best thing for a child to do is respond to God at the earliest age possible. A survey of thousands of seminary students shows that most of them came to God as little children. Two mature preachers with whom I am acquainted started preaching when they were in grade school. Never discount how significant it is to begin with God and spend life's entire day with Him.

In direct contrast to the integrity of Samuel stand the perverse sons of Eli, who contaminate the very temple of God with their greed and immorality. They skim off the offerings and seduce the young women coming to church. Eli cannot or will not control them. When he learns of their death and the capture of the ark of the covenant, he falls over dead. This leaves a gap in the holy history of Israel, and Samuel steps up to begin a life somewhere between the role of a judge and a prophet. He is the man in the middle during the transition of Israel's life—from what was to what would be. This is never an easy place to stand because the ground can shift. Nevertheless, he stayed the course.

The fate of Eli's sons has given the church a reminder that should not be overlooked: The Christian faith cannot be inherited. Salvation does not come to families, but to individuals. Christian history is littered with second generations of children who never embraced the Christ of their parents. Lost destinies, aborted ministries, unfulfilled promises, and total depravity have not been strangers to the children of some servants of God. The Christian faith must be a personal reality, or it will be nothing at all. Faith is not automatically woven into the DNA of a child. Every individual must come to living faith by a personal response.

We cannot know how much Eli tried to pass the faith on to his sons. What we do know is that at the place of worship in Shiloh, at the very door of the assembly, the sons of the man of God rejected all He stood for and what their father had given his life for.

Samuel is the last of the judges and the first of the major prophets. He anointed the first two kings of Israel. Later rabbis considered him every bit the equal of Moses in his stature and life. We will consider his life in this book just because he lived in the in-between times. He looks back to the best devotion of the past, extending all the way back to Abraham a thousand years before. He looks forward to the future of Israel. On the far horizon of that history is Jesus, King of Kings. Samuel pivots between what was and what is in the holy history of God's people.

Samuel provides living proof of how important God's individual servant can be, even though it may not look like it at the time. Who would have guessed that the boy at Shiloh living with old Eli would become the mouthpiece for God to the nation?

We never know whom God may use. Dr. Gardner Taylor wanted to be a lawyer. Billy Graham was the son of a dairy farmer. Dr. J. Alfred Smith blew a horn in a band yet walked off the bandstand into national leadership as a minister. Who knows whom God may use? Maybe you?

When Samuel was still a youth at Shiloh, the dreaded Philistines, a vicious people on the fringe of Israel, conquered and subjected the people of Israel. As an ultimate insult they captured the ark of the covenant and carried it away. They acted out of blatant arrogance, as if they could cart off the God of Israel. For 20 years the Israelites lived under that humiliating subjection. As a grown judge/prophet/general, Samuel leads Israel in a battle that decisively defeats the Philistines. Samuel erects a memorial stone and peace follows.

Serving God rarely occurs without a battle. Faith fights. Battles rage within the believer and outside the believer. The Old Testament comprises stories of one battle after another for the people of God.

Samuel initially wanted his sons to succeed him. The Israelites, however, clamored for a king. Samuel warned them sternly about the consequences of having a king, but the people clamored all the more. Finally Samuel anointed Saul, the son of Kish, as king, an event that led to one of the great disappointments of Samuel's life. Saul turned out to be a disobedient nut case, a paranoid schizophrenic. He was a colossal disappointment.

After Saul's disobedient acts, God ordered Samuel to anoint another king. In an unlikely ancient equivalent of "American Idol" ("Find A King"), Samuel looks at the most likely candidates and selects the most unlikely, a little shepherd boy named David. Thus began one of the famous reigns of history. Before the retirement of Samuel he gathered Israel together for a closing sermon. He warned them again about idolatry and what they would face in the future since they demanded a king. Then he went into retirement.

Be careful when God gives you what you want but He knows you should not have. Such belongs to the mystery of the providence of God. The life of Samuel suggests a mystery in our prayers. Sometimes you may pester God until He says, "OK. You want it that much? You got it. And you will live with it." We will consider this permissive will of the God who lets you have what you want even though He knows it will not work for you. How the will of God works is often a mystery wrapped up in a puzzle.

According to the rabbis Samuel died at 52, an old

age for that time and place. Yet he was not really gone. He made a famous final posthumous appearance when a troubled and depressed Saul requested the witch at Endor to summon Samuel up from Sheol, the realm of the dead. The witch held a séance, and to her surprise, it worked. The deceased indeed came back, to the abject terror of both Saul and the witch. Samuel delivers a final withering denunciation to Saul and goes back to the bosom of Abraham.

The Bible consistently warns against the practice of magical arts. The Word of God never denies that a dark world of evil exists just beyond the visible world. It warns again and again to stay away because dabbling in the occult is not just a game, but a sinkhole. You may get more than you wanted when you go there.

This thumbnail of Samuel's life just gives you a bare outline. The messages that follow will explore these themes and more. You may be living in the in-between right now. Between one home and another. Between one career and another. Between one relationship and another. Between past certainty and future uncertainty. Let's walk together through the life of Samuel to see what it is like to live in between. ✜

CHAPTER TWO

A Follower's Follow-through

(1 Samuel 1:21-28)

ON SEPTEMBER 5, 1987, DR. BEN CARSON awakened and began his day just like many others—kneeling beside his bed and praying to God. On this day awaiting him at Johns Hopkins Hospital were Patrick and Benjamin Binder from Germany, Siamese twins conjoined at the cranium. It would be Carson's feat that day to surgically separate them, an operation that had never been successfully achieved in medical history. The neurosurgeon got on his knees and gave to God what God had already given to him—his hands. He prayed, "God, give me wisdom, and give me guidance." For 28 consecutive hours, with intermittent breaks to discuss the surgery with other physicians, he operated on those twins. Thousands of interlocked veins had to be untangled and repaired, and he worked to the point of exhaustion. From his own lips, Dr. Carson testified that after he had prayed again, a power outside of himself invigorated him, enabling him to follow through with what he had prayed for that previous morning.

Ben Carson's prayer life did not begin when he was

elected elder of the Seventh-day Adventist Church, nor when he started teaching a Bible class at his home church while on staff at Johns Hopkins. It went all the way back to his days in the ghettos of Detroit as a fifth-grader growing up with his brother Curtis. One day he had brought home a failing report card. His single mother Sonya wisely picked up that card, turned off the television, and demanded that her boys read two books a week. What is ironic is that Sonya Carson herself could not read because she only had a third-grade education. She would make them write a report at the end of the week about the two books they had read, and then she would take a pen and make corrections in the margin. No one knew how she accomplished this feat, but she did.

Ben Carson said that what he remembers most about his mother is this prayer: "Lord, give me wisdom, and give me guidance." She prayed her sons through their elementary, middle, and high school years, as well as their college and graduate studies. In an interview Dr. Carson said, "People have often called me gifted. I am not gifted. All I am is an instrument that has been used in the hands of God, and I learned that from my mother, who prayed, 'Lord, give me wisdom, and Lord, give me guidance.' And the Lord directed all of my paths." For weal or for woe, there is an intensity and immensity in the prayers of a mother.

We are not astonished in the least when reading about the life of Byron to discover that his mother was bad tempered, ill mannered, and violent. Neither does it surprise us that Nero's mother was a murderess. On the other hand, we are not astounded at all after reading the poems of Sir Walter Scott to discover that his mother also loved words, language, and poetry. When we sing the songs or listen to the sermons of John and Charles Wesley, or read about the lives of St. Augustine, Chrysostom, or St. Basil the Great, we are not at all amazed to discover that their mothers were also religious devotees of the faith.

Eighteenth-century British philosopher Lord Shaftesbury once said, "Give me a generation of Christian mothers, and I will undertake to change the whole face of society in 12 months." Something significant happens when a mother gives herself over to prayer on behalf of her children.

When Douglas MacArthur attended West Point, his mother got a place to live just outside the citadel walls where she could watch his dormitory. She would check to see if his lights were on late at night and if they were on early in the morning—just to make sure that he was staying diligent with his studies. In short, we never should underestimate the influence and power of a caring mother.

We come now to another mother and son in another time. If ever there was a child conceived in prayer, it was he. This godly woman made a commitment to her Lord that the boy would serve Him all the days of his life if He would only grant him life. His name was Samuel, and as his name indicates, he indeed was a gift from God.

Samuel was a person who lived in the in-between times. He lived his life between two prayers, those of his mother at the beginning of the book and David's at the end. Moreover, he lived between the times of the judges and the coming of the kings—in between theocracy and monarchy, good and evil, life and death, the past and the future. In every sense of the word, Samuel was a man who lived, in the words of Eugene Peterson, at the "millennium mid-post."

Faithfulness that follows through remains faithful in the face of disappointments.

Whatever details we know about Samuel's childhood relate to his mother, Hannah. Hannah was married to Elkanah, a prominent businessman from the hill country of Ramah. They were a family deeply committed to participating in the annual pilgrimage to the shrine in Shiloh. At that tabernacle they would offer their prayers, worship, and sacrifices to God.

The dilemma that afflicts Hannah is her barrenness,

the inability to bear children. In Old Testament times, a woman would rather be called anything else other than barren. "Barren" was the word used to describe a woman who was not whole or complete; in other words, she was not really usable. She was only meant to be thrown aside because she was considered worthless.

Barrenness was considered a curse from God. No wonder Elizabeth shouted out when John the Baptist was born, "God has taken away my disgrace." Those must have been the same words that Sarah would speak when Isaac was born or Rebekah would speak about her twins, Jacob and Esau. In fact, the barrenness of these mothers of the Israelite nation was significant in that their ability to finally bear children was a sign of the grace and favor of God toward His people.

Unfortunately, barrenness was always blamed on the woman. Yet this was the same man who had been with Peninnah. Perhaps something was wrong with Elkanah. On the other hand, it could have been the wrong time for Hannah to conceive a child. Could this in itself have been a secondary cause? Nevertheless, there is nothing secondary about this story; the only primary cause is God Himself. Verse 5 says, "The Lord had closed her womb." Clearly God is at work behind the scenes, about to make something happen.

Even the names of the two wives are a play on words.

"Hannah" means "charming," but "Peninnah" means "fecund; prolific."The literal interpretation signifies that Elkanah loved Hannah but he used Peninnah to make up for what Hannah was incapable of producing.

And yet, in the face of her barrenness, Hannah never stopped going to the shrine to offer up her verbal praise and worship, which was her sacrifice to God. She did not allow her disappointments or bad situations—what she did not have—to stop her from trusting, relying, and depending on God. As a result, God honored the faithfulness of Hannah.

Not one of us has escaped the vise-like talons of disappointment—not even some of the greatest Christians, past and present.

- The missionary William Carey experienced enormous disappointments again and again that were beyond comprehension. Fighting against all odds in India, he shipped a printing press there. After translating the Bible into Hindi, he was prepared to print it when the press burned down. Carey cried as the ink melted around his feet. *Yet, he remained faithful to God.*
- Joni Erickson Tada became a quadriplegic due to a diving accident. She remains faithful as a Christian witness through her writing and speaking.

Perhaps you follow God based on what He does for you. If He does not appear to deliver on His promises to you, you stop praying, worshipping, praising, and attending church services. However, that is not not faithful "follow-ship." You must faithfully follow the Lord by trusting, serving, and worshipping Him—even when you do not know what the outcome or answer will be.

Faithfulness that follows through remains faithful in the face of loss and ridicule.

But then that faithfulness goes beyond disappointment, stretching itself to follow God even in the face of loss and ridicule. The other wife in this story irritated poor Hannah unmercifully. Peninnah used her fertility to lord it over her rival by ridiculing her, and it was enough to break the heart of Hannah. Every day Hannah wept so much that she could not even eat. The Scripture says that she wept "inconsolably" to the point that even Elkanah said, "Don't I treat you better than 10 sons?" He did not understand her basic need. She wanted to have a baby boy. Yet, in the face of loss and ridicule, Hannah still faithfully followed God. She still went to church, and she still prayed.

Recently that great monument of Dr. Martin Luther King on the plaza in Washington, D.C., was unveiled. Those who reflect upon Dr. King's life inevitably consider how he had to serve God in the face of loss and ridicule. On the one hand were those who supported his nonviolent philosophy for racial reconciliation, and on the other hand were those who opposed him because of his protests against the Vietnam War. In every sense, when that man died, the valedictory given for him was this: "He was a person who died in the middle."

At times in your life, that is where you will find yourself. You will still have to trust God and faithfully serve Him in the middle—in the known and the unknown, the have and the have not.

Faithfulness may lead you to seek God with an intensity that might be misunderstood.

In verses 8 and 9 Hannah was sitting around the table, and then she got up. Eli, whose eyesight was faulty, observed her when she stood up. She opened her mouth and said this prayer in verses 10 and 11—that God would remember her and open her womb. If He did, she would give her son back to Him. There is no indication that a boy would be born, but that is what she prayed for and believed.

Many Christians have held Hannah in such high regard that they have almost deified her. But they praise Hannah too much at times because she is uttering a prayer of bargaining with God—always the grounds of naïveté and superficiality. She is seeking a culturally defined end rather than understanding God's true end for her life. In other words, she is trying to resolve that burden her society is placing on her.

This temptation to bargain with God has happened to all of us. We have all been sophomoric, superficial, and naïve with our prayers. We have often prayed for what we wanted for ourselves, rather than praying for the larger picture of God's will in the world. Nevertheless, biblical theology at its highest allows God to help us establish the end so we can then offer ourselves as the means.

So, all Hannah is thinking about now is herself—not the shrine, Eli, God, or anybody else. She is just telling God that if He blesses her so that she can get her revenge on Peninnah for her harassment, then He can have what He gives to her. Indeed, she is praying out of naïveté.

At least Hannah recognized that her infertility was not medical or biological, but theological. If it had been medical, she would have sought the advice of the local physicians. Yet she decided not to do that. Instead Hannah went to God because she recognized that what was wrong with her was theological, not biological.

Many of us get upset with God when we try to parallel our lives with people in the Scriptures—and fail. For the Scriptures to be interpreted correctly, however, certain passages must be interpreted either descriptively or prescriptively. In this case, this is a descriptive passage, not prescriptive. That is, just because we pray what Hannah prayed does not mean our outcome will be just like Hannah's.

Descriptively, this story is recorded in the Scriptures to remind us that this is a theological issue. In other words, God Himself is involved in the context of this story. This is more about God than it is about Hannah, Elkanah, or Peninnah. God is trying to get His way on planet Earth because at this time the world is in between and He needs somebody to serve Him in between the good and the bad, the up and the down, the in and the out.

Verse 12 says that Hannah "kept on praying." At first, in verse 11, she is praying verbally. By the time she gets to verse 12, however, she has run out of words. Now she is praying in her heart. Eli looks at her and notices that her mouth is moving, but no words are coming out.

At that very moment, Hannah is praying with such intensity that when Eli sees her, he mistakenly concludes that she is intoxicated. She informs him that she is not drunk; instead, she is pouring out her heart to God.

Consider the words used to describe her disposition during her intense praying. According to verses 10, 11, 15, and 16, she was downhearted and deeply troubled, awash in deep anguish, grief, and misery. Now think about your most intense moments, such as trying to get a ticket to a sold-out event or attempting to get a celebrity autograph. Do your prayers to God ever reach that same level of intensity? If you have never been there, just keep on living. When you continue to pray but cannot find the right words, all you can do then is close your eyes. Your mouth may be moving, but nothing is coming out. All the while, however, God is working inside your heart.

This is an important verse in 1 Samuel: "Man looks at the outward appearance, but only God looks at the heart" (16:7). Eli could pass judgment upon Hannah, but at the same time he refuses to make an accusation against his own sons, the corrupt priests Hophni and Phineas. Yet he wants to call Hannah drunk and out of control because she appears to be one who has been imbibing wine.

In Acts 2 on the Day of Pentecost, another similar mistake was made by myopic religious people. The Holy Spirit had been poured out on the early church, and the critics accused the congregation of being drunk. Joel 2:28-29, the text Peter preached from, prophesied that when the Holy Spirit falls on the church, young men would see visions and the old men would dream dreams. Young women would announce God's good news to the world when the Spirit came upon the church. People would be in control but out of control at the same time. They would no longer be drunk with wine; instead, they would be filled with the Holy Spirit.

When you reach that level of intensity with God, people will start calling you fanatical, strange, and peculiar. They will say, "Look at you, trying to act all holy." "No," you could reply, "but I have been so unholy for such a long time." Why should you not say that? You can rightfully tell them, "It is time for me to live under the influence and power of the Holy Spirit." If you keep following the Lord with that kind of intensity, He will surely lead you into a life of faithfulness.

That is what happened to modern-day missionary Frank Laubach. He claimed that he wanted to live every hour and minute of the day with his mind on Jesus. His critics said he could never do it. But he was not trying to do it for them; it was something *he* wanted to do. In his book, *Letters by a Modern Mystic*, Laubach reports that he did just that in the Philippines. One day, with everything he did, he kept his mind on Jesus. During his workday, whether he was typing or teaching, his mind was on Jesus. People accused him of being a crazy fanatic.

It is amazing how often people say you are crazy if your mind is fixed on Jesus. Nobody makes that statement if you are drunk or high on drugs. Nobody says that if you are acting like a fool in the middle of the street. But all of a sudden they say you are a fanatic if your mind is stayed on Jesus. Yet, every now and then, out of the 24 hours in a day, we ought to be able to give the Lord some time when our mind is intensely fixed on Him.

Faithfulness finds vindication from unexpected sources.

Eli observed the method of Hannah's prayer without understanding her motives for praying. After she corrects him, the same voice that accused her in one breath is the same voice that vindicated her in the next breath. Eli said, "You are drunk," in one breath, but then in the next breath, he said, "However the Lord of Israel will bless you, let it be yours." In one breath he is pointing his finger, and with the next breath he is lifting her up.

God has the power to change your critics into your biggest supporters. The very people who accused you on one hand turn around and praise your name on the other hand. The same individuals who put you down are the same ones who will give you a hand to lift you up. The same people who tried to hurt you are the same ones who will turn around and bless you.

Dr. Randall O'Brien, the former executive vice president of Baylor and the current president of Carson-Newman College, told this story at a Truett Seminary student gathering. When he was serving as a pastor at a church in Oklahoma City, the Imperial Wizard of the Ku Klux Klan—and this wasn't in the '40s or '50s—threatened the life of an African-American pastor in the city. Because this local head of the KKK was such an extreme racist and bigot who also had the power behind him to commit this horrible deed, they believed he would do it. Do you know what happened to this Klansman? He showed up at church, and something happened: the Holy Spirit reached him.

And then, the story gets better than that. Just like when Paul the apostle got converted, there were some people who refused to believe the Klansman had been redeemed, so he needed a Barnabas. This person who became the absolver of the Imperial Wizard was not a white man, but an African-American pastor. That minister, like Eli, had to change his opinion and validate the work of God in the life of another unlikely person. The former Ku Klux Klan leader went from church to church, giving his testimony about the power and redemption of the Lord Jesus Christ.

The worst rascals in the world can be completely turned around if the Holy Spirit gets a hold of them. (Those of you who falsely judge them should be careful here. The only people who refuse to forgive are the same ones who have not experienced forgiveness for themselves.) God will save the unlikeliest people. Testimonies are not given by nice people, but by those who are branded by our society as the worst. Some people see them give their lives to Jesus and then say, "If God can save them, then I stand a chance."

I want God to save the worst people He can find. We must bring the rascals whom no one else in our society wants into the church and watch God save them. We want those who say, "There is no hope for me." Then it will be our great privilege to let them know that the Lord is able to vindicate them.

In the church, we have ex-this and ex-that. If it had not been for the Lord, who heard the earnest prayers of our mothers and grandmothers, we would not be here right now. God will lift us up and liberate us. He will turn our lives around.

Faithfulness does follow through.

It is important to follow through. In every sport, whether it is baseball, tennis, or golf, the lack of a good follow-through ruins the game. When Jack Welch was the CEO of General Electric, he was legendary for following through on every single detail of the scores of visits he made to GE companies. From Sunbeam mixers to jet engines, he always followed through on every observation, detail, and order.

Against all odds, Sir Ernest Shackleton followed through on his promise to return and rescue his men who were trapped in the ice during a polar expedition. Because of his tireless heroics, no lives were lost—despite a seemingly impossible situation.

God favors those who follow through. Hannah prayed a prayer and made a vow before her son was ever born. When Samuel was born, she carried out her promise and sent him to live his life at the shrine in Shiloh. God had remembered her, and she remembered God. The beautiful part of this story is that God took Hannah's situation, with all her self-centered desire, and once again brought something good out of the less than perfect. He met Hannah where she was in her cultural captivity and nonetheless brought forth one of the truly great men in all of the Old Testament. This offers a basis of hope for all of us—that God can take just about anything and do just about everything with it.

We can only imagine what it must have been like for Hannah to turn loose of what she waited so long to get. But she faithfully followed through anyway, and God showed favor in her life. When her son was turned over to Eli in Shiloh, the Scripture says these words: "He ministered before the Lord" (2:18). Samuel ministered before the Lord as a very young child. Every year

Hannah spent time weaving an ephod, a linen priestly garment, to fit her son as he grew.

We must be careful about how we regard our children and their future. If we would just live godly lifestyles of faith and faithfulness in front of them, we do not know what God may have in store for their lives. You may want your son to be a football or basketball player, or a star entertainer or academician. While you desire all of that for your son, make sure you teach him about God. He will receive your teaching according to how you serve God. There comes a time when you have to live faithfully before God as an example to your children.

In verse 26, it says that Samuel ministered, but he also grew in the stature and favor of God. He grew physically, but he also grew morally and intellectually and spiritually.

Those words sound familiar to us when we study the Gospels. At the age of 12, Jesus had gone to the temple with His parents. While Jesus was there, they left and He was lagging behind in the temple courtyard, holding court with the religious scholars, the philosophers, and the academicians of His day. When He spoke, they said, "We have never heard anyone speak like this before. This boy is way beyond His years. He knows things that we have not even heard about. He is teaching *us*." Mary and Joseph came back and said, "It is time to go home." Jesus said, "I must be about My Father's business now."

The next verse says that Mary tucked these things in her heart.

Eighteen years later, He would get up, dust Himself off, and go to the Jordan, where He would stand in line and then get baptized. His ministry would soon be inaugurated and baptized, not just in the waters of the Jordan, but in the desert wilderness. There, Satan would try to get Him to renege on following through. But Jesus did not quit there. He faithfully followed God and stayed with His Father's business in the wilderness and throughout His entire ministry, even when His disciples misunderstood Him. When they tried to persuade Him to circumvent His plan, He just kept on faithfully following God.

Jesus was not a robot; He did not have to go through with God's plan. Following His Father was a choice that He made. Nobody made Him do it. In fact, when Jesus prayed in the Garden of Gethsemane, He could have turned around right there. But He must have thought, *Well, if I do that, no one will ever get saved. They never will experience grace.* Even though He pleaded with the Father, "If it is possible, take this cup from me," He added, "Not My will, but Thy will be done." And so, Jesus kept on being faithful, even to the cross. He followed through until that moment when He said, "It is finished!" He finished what He started, and He sealed it when He got up on Resurrection Morning.

You may have made a promise to God. You said, "Lord, if You bless me, if You heal me, if You deliver my children, if You set me free, I promise to serve You." But you have been slack about keeping your promise every week. Instead, you are moving to the margin. If you are farther away from God today than you were two years ago, you already know that you are going backwards. But since God has kept His end of the prayer, you also ought to keep your end now.

The Lord has been so faithful to you. In fact, He has not missed one day of waking you up. He starts you on your way. He puts a shelter over your head and food in your stomach. He has not missed one day. Since the Lord has been this faithful to you, then today is the day you ought to be faithful to Him. Let this be the day when you say, "I will follow Jesus. No turning back!" ❖

CHAPTER THREE

Present and Accounted For
(1 Samuel 3:8-10, 19)

At the age of 30, George W. Truett launched his pastoral ministry at First Baptist Church of Dallas. His future was bright, but five months after he moved to Dallas, a devastating tragedy struck that almost caused him to leave the ministry.

In February 1898 Truett went on a quail hunting trip with Jim Arnold, who was the chief of the Dallas Police Department and a member of his First Baptist congregation. They took a train ride together to Cleburne, Texas, to go and quail-hunt on the Boyd farm upon the invitation extended to them by George Baines, a member of First Baptist Church in Cleburne. When the three met, they began their day of hunting quail, but it was a fruitless quest. Truett wanted to return to Dallas, but the others persuaded him to stay and try again the next day. After the noon hour had come and no quail had been shot, Truett wanted to go back to Dallas, and Baines wanted to go back to Cleburne. But Chief Arnold, wanting his pastor to shoot at least one quail, insisted that they try just one more time.

Around 3:30, Baines was hunting by himself and decided to return to the farmhouse. Arnold and Truett were hunting together on the other side. Suddenly Baines heard two gunshots within ten seconds apart. A few minutes later, he saw Truett running in from the field, hat in hand. When Baines ran out to meet him, the first words that came from Truett's mouth were, "I have shot Jim Arnold." The second shot Baines had heard occurred when Truett shifted his shotgun from one arm to the other, discharging the gun and wounding Arnold in the right leg.

After wrapping Arnold's wound, they took the police chief to the doctor. Arnold tried his best to persuade Pastor Truett to go back to Dallas to inform the chief's wife about the accident, but Truett refused to leave. Baines said he had never seen a more miserable person after an accident than George Truett, "and this added to the captain's pain." Finally Truett went back to Dallas to convey the messages.

While Truett was on his way home, Arnold grew concerned about his heart, so he asked two doctors to examine him. After the physicians determined that Arnold was well enough to be moved, Baines and the doctors accompanied Arnold on a train back to Dallas. On that Saturday morning after Baines had returned to Cleburne, a telegram arrived for him that said Jim

Arnold had died from a heart attack.

Truett was, to say the least, a human wreck. Those from the city of Dallas and the First Baptist Church of Dallas reported that they heard him walking back and forth in his home crying out, "My times are in Your hand!" Buried deep within a psychological malaise, Truett said to his wife Josephine, "I shall never again enter into the pulpit." Those who knew Truett, along with those who wrote about him, often talked about the incident. Some said that he preached with a tear in his throat—that he never smiled again. That may be a stretch of the imagination, but it illustrates the seriousness of the situation.

But then something happened that pulled Truett out of his paralyzing depression. One night he awoke three separate times and told Josephine that he dreamed Jesus had visited him in his room and stood by his bedside. Jesus told him, "George, be not afraid. You are My man from now on." This was the turning point for Pastor George W. Truett, and he decided to continue preaching in the pulpit of First Baptist Church. George W. Truett was a servant of the Lord who responded to His call. Indeed, he was present and accounted for.

In 1923 the German philosopher Martin Buber wrote a classic book entitled *I-Thou*, a radical assessment of the way humans relate to each other and to God. According to Buber, human beings may adopt one of two attitudes toward the world, God, and each other: *I-thou* or *I-it*. I-thou involves a relation of subject to subject, while I-it refers to a relation of subject to object. In the I-thou relationship, people never reduce individuals down to specificities or isolated quantities. Instead, they see others as unique gifts from God—that is, engaged through dialogue, conversation, and oneness.

When people look at others through the I-it lens, not only do they perceive them as specific, isolated quantities, but rather as impersonal cogs in a machine. Thus, Buber would say that it is quite easy to mistreat a person when you fail to see him as a person, but as an "it" or a thing.

Whenever we look upon a man as an "it," we can lynch him, drag him behind a car, or mistreat or exploit him. So the reality is that even as Christians, we can become so spiritual we forget that God has not called us to devalue other human beings. At any rate, we must realize that we are not in an I-it relationship, but an I-thou relationship.

Some of us live on the superficial I-it level. We never meet people—just their position, title, credentials, or sociology. Whenever we do that, however, we not only demean them, but we reduce ourselves as well. We can only be whole people when we look at others through the eyes of the Lord Jesus Christ.

I-it persons often can be found within the walls of the church. They are happy because they still have a job; unemployment has not affected them in the least. They assume that they are a little better than those who have lost their jobs. Because they have a new car and have received a raise to get that new house so they do not have to live in an apartment anymore, they think that their lives merely consist of the abundance of things they possess. However, it just might be that the things they possess *possess* them. Anybody can be happy when he or she has a job and has money in the bank. Anybody can pray when one's friends are there. But how do they behave when all of that is taken away?

People tend to act holy and spiritual when things are going well. When things turn out badly, however, they start bargaining with God: "Lord, if You do this . . ." They should rather say, "Lord, I am responsible, even if everything is going wrong in my life. I am not about to point my finger in Your face—as good as You have been to me and all the times You have tried to prevent me from crossing over the line."

This passage in 1 Samuel assures us that at the heart of reality there is not an IT but a THOU, Someone who is more like a person than anything else we can imagine. *When God calls you by name, He anticipates receiving a personal response from you.* He expects you to say, "Present. Mark me present. I am here today."

God calls you when you are in the place you need to be.

There is a big word theologians use to characterize the ways of God: omnipresent. It means that He is everywhere at the same time. He is everlasting to everlasting. He is always going where He is coming from. He is *omni*present.

Yet there are places that even the omnipresent God can access with more facility than others. Certainly God can speak to people at the bar during happy hour between apple martinis or at the game in some sports venue, but those are not the most accessible places for God to speak to them. God speaks in places and spaces that have been specifically designated for Him by those who are centered in His purposes.

Many of you have a special place in your home where you meet with God. This space, regardless of how many guests visit you, is set apart for you and God. This is not a place where you have phone conversations or read good books. When you need to talk to God, you have arranged this place with Him to be your spiritual rendezvous. This is *your* special space where you can be alone with Him.

Modern-day Celtic spiritualists have brought back the ancient concept of what they call the "thin space." In simple terms, this is the place where the veil between this world and the other one is so thin that the other world appears very near. Yet this space cannot be accessed through the five senses. Instead, this involves a spiritual dynamic of the sixth sense. This is the moment when you are praying and you unexplainably move to a dimension that is neither emotional nor mental. You just know in your heart that you have gone to another spiritual dimension of prayer and worship where you can reach out and touch God.

This is nothing new or strange. For hundreds of years, Irish spiritualists have been talking about this "thin space" because humanity has always been concerned with the otherness of life. All of these questions interest conscientious people: What is beyond the clouds? What about heaven? Where does God preside? Where is His domain? Then again, if people do not understand a dimension of "upness," they often wonder about the dimension of "downness." Is there a hell? Is there an abyss? Are there isolations for violations?

So, when you have arranged a special place to meet God, you have an opportunity to reach into that spiritual otherness where you can pray, sit still, and read the Scriptures. Something so unbelievable happens there that you know no one but God could have done it—otherness. He may give you fresh revelation about spiritual concepts you have heard taught many times. When God breathes on those very same words, you hear them in a way you have never heard them before, and your life is forever changed as a result.

Samuel's thin place was in Shiloh. In that place, he heard God speak because he was where he was supposed to be. Similarly, God could reach us if we were in the place He directed us to be. People will often ask us, "Did the Holy Spirit bring you to such and such church?" We can honestly answer yes because if He did not lead us, we would never have gotten out of bed. We do not go to church because we think the pastor will preach a great sermon; instead, we go because the Holy Spirit tells us to go. The Holy Spirit knows the place where we are supposed to be because He knows what we need to hear.

If you are listening in the right place, God calls as long as it takes for you to hear Him.

We should all be thankful that God does not set a limit on the number of calls He makes to us. God called Samuel three times by name until he answered. Similarly, God repeatedly called Moses until he answered the call to lead the Israelites out of their bondage in Egypt.

In the Gospels, Jesus called the four most mentioned disciples—Peter, Andrew, James, and John. He called them once in the desert by the Jordan River when they were following John the Baptist (John 1). In Mark 1:16-20, when they were busy about their job of fishing in the Sea of Galilee, He called them again. They promptly lay down their nets, left their employer Zebedee, and followed Him.

Even though these disciples followed Jesus to the crucifixion, they did not stay with Him after that. In John 21 they thought Jesus was dead and gone, so they went back to their profession that Jesus had called them from when He first met them. Out of the richness of His mercy, Jesus called them to follow Him—again by the Sea of Galilee.

In the same way, God loves you so much that when you go back to the activities you were involved in before He called you, He will stand on the shore and keep on calling you by His grace.

This triple call of the apostles underscores the necessity of listening for the voice of God and understanding that voice when He calls. Fortunately, God persists in making His calls to us. The biography of Christian author and apologist C.S. Lewis demonstrates this unfailing patience of God. The Lord began calling Lewis when he was a little boy embittered by the death of his mother and the emotional distance of his father. God kept calling him through the experiences of joy, His ubiquitous presence in nature, faithful Christian friends such as J.R.R. Tolkien, and the falsity of all other experiences that fell short of what God held for him.

Faithful people may help you understand the voice of God.

Samuel has been called, and he thinks that it is Eli calling him. But Eli tells him that he was not the one who called him. What makes the call more mysterious is verse 1: "In those days, the word of the Lord was rare. There were not many visions." That is, God was not speaking very much because the people were not embracing what He had already said. Now God finds somebody at Shiloh in a thin place where He can reach from one side of the veil to the other.

Eli told Samuel what to say the next time he heard his name called: "Speak, Lord, for Your servant is listening." It took Eli to build a bridge between Samuel and God. Eli acted in the role of what is known today as the "spiritual director," a wise, mature mentor who helped Samuel recognize the voice of God.

Throughout both the Hebrew and the Christian Scriptures, we find people seeking spiritual counsel. The Queen of Sheba sought out the wisdom of

Solomon. Jesus gave us examples in his conversations with Nicodemus, the woman at the well, and in the ongoing development of Peter and the other disciples. In the early church, people flocked to hermits in the desert for spiritual counsel. Across the centuries we find striking examples in some Irish monks, some German Benedictine nuns, Charles de Foucault, Teresa of Avila, John of the Cross, Francis de Sales, and others.

In short, spiritual direction involves a conversation with someone who has had spiritual experiences through which they are able to hear yours and guide you into possibly hearing what God might be saying. Even though no one can ever know all of what God is saying, he or she can help you find the right direction by letting you know how to pray and what to read. But how are you going to know that if you are never in the position to hear God in the first place and do not have anybody to guide you?

In our local churches God has surrounded us with people who will help us understand what He is saying. So many Christians today are in trouble because they do not have a pastor who guides them on a spiritual level. The radio and TV evangelists they often listen to may be able to help them, but they cannot personally shepherd them.

Flocks do not get shepherded by remote control.

When shepherds are with their sheep, they know where they are supposed to go. That is how God set up the church. Many Christians are confused because they are debating with God over what He has already established.

God sends truth the way He wants to send it. If you are in darkness, you should not care what your spiritual mentor looks like or where he has been. If they have been to the same place you are trying to go and can help you get out of darkness into His marvelous light, then you must go with them.

God vindicates you when you are present and accounted for.

Verse 19 says that the Lord was with Samuel as he grew up. Samuel is not a special person with supernatural gifts; he is just somebody with whom God has spoken. The verse continues, " . . . and none of his words fell to the ground." What that means is that his words were full of wisdom and insight and able to do what they were supposed to accomplish. His prophecies were marked with such uncanny maturity that God used them to build bridges between Himself and the people. How Samuel arrives at this place by growing and maturing in His relationship with God is significant in itself.

Typically, there are two ways we encounter God through conversion. One is the process of evolution, and the other is revolution. Evolution involves growing and developing into a spiritually mature person. On the other hand, there are times when individuals experience a radical revolution in their lives, such as Paul's Damascus Road experience.

The example God provides us in Samuel teaches us that what might be good for Paul or the prodigal son in the pigpen who comes to his senses after a period of spiritual lethargy might not be what He desires for some of us. Perhaps God is putting up detours to prevent us from experiencing a life crisis. We may not have to go through a divorce, loss of job, or nervous breakdown to come to God. Instead, we can be like Samuel and just grow because we are in the right place in the right space.

The well-known pastor Harry Emerson Fosdick said, "When Samuel came to God, he crossed the river at the narrow place." This was the place where the water was not turbulent, but still and calm. Samuel's life with God was one of continuity and steady growth rather than the crisis-after-crisis pattern that is getting so much attention nowadays. This is important to note, for what could be called "the Damascus Road syndrome" is far more colorful, and if we are not careful, can get elevated into the single norm of all Christian conversion encounters.

The way Samuel matured in God is a good corrective at this point, for early in his pilgrimage he began encountering the Mystery and saying yes. He did not need the kind of radical about-face that someone like the prodigal son in Jesus' parable had to undergo.

This is not to imply that there was anything mechanical or automatic about Samuel's walk with God. He did have to decide for himself at each juncture. When the still, small voice of God impinged upon his consciousness, it was Samuel—not Eli—who had to answer. Yet his answer was affirmative: "Speak, Lord, for Your servant is listening." This became the pattern for his whole life, which is undoubtedly the reason why his efforts counted for so much and none of his words "fell to the ground."

Eventually the entire nation came to acknowledge the quiet spirituality of this aged prophet. Their recognition enabled Samuel to maintain his dignity throughout the difficult times of his long life. In this passage, God Himself authenticated His eternal promise to Samuel.

Similarly, God often uses someone in the crowd to step up and defend you at a moment's notice, and you do not even know it. He will vindicate you because you are present and accounted for.

Some time after Robert Robinson, the writer of the hymn "Come, Thou Fount of Every Blessing," penned its well-known words, he walked away from God. For him, life had just ended up nowhere. One day he hitched a ride on a carriage, and a little old lady sitting next to him with a book open started singing his hymn. He began singing it with her, and she asked him if he knew the song. He told her that he had written it. Then he said, "I needed to hear that song to remember these words: 'Prone to wander, Lord I feel it/Prone to leave the God I love.' "

Every one of us is wired that way, but the good news is that when you stray away, God will call you back. When He does, all you have to do is respond, "Speak Lord, for Your servant is listening." ✤

CHAPTER FOUR

Choosing the Second Best
(1 Samuel 8:1-10, 19-22)

ON OCTOBER 14, 1942, EDDIE RICKENBACKER, one of the founders of the now defunct Eastern Airlines, was a passenger on the B-17D *Flying Fortress*, flying over the Central South Pacific during World War II. He had been given presidential orders to review the living conditions and military operations in the Pacific theater of operations, and then deliver a secret message to General Douglas MacArthur. Upon completion of those tasks, he flew throughout the Central Pacific to refuel at Kanton Island.

While checking the coordinates and navigational instruments and monitoring the time, the captain and crew noticed that even though they should have been seeing a tiny island, nothing was there but water. Later they would learn that because of a pre-existing condition resulting from some mishap, the entire navigational system was corrupted by what was known as systemic bias, which caused it to emit the wrong readings from the beginning. When the captain programmed the navigational direction, the systemic bias inside the instrument read one degree off, meaning that from the very take-off, the farther they flew, the farther off-course they would fly.

By the time they were supposed to land, they had strayed hundreds of miles away from their destination because their navigational instrument was off by one degree. They had to ditch the plane in the Central Pacific. Rickenbacker's story actually became one of those legendary military-hero epics that recounted how his crew of eight survived the dangers of the Pacific Ocean.

That "systemic bias" not only affects aircraft, but also nations and people. From the very beginning, we may program our lives toward one place, but because of a preexisting systemic bias inside of us (sin), we are misdirected from the very beginning. Despite our best efforts, we may choose one place to go and end up somewhere else. This leads us to that moment when we say, "If I had to do it all over again . . ." Choices that we made some 10, 20, or 30 years ago we would bypass today. But due to this systemic bias that programmed us in the wrong way, we made some bad choices.

You must be aware of this systemic bias because God may allow you to have something that you have asked for that He really does not want you to have. That is a haunting reality—to assume that you can push your way and impose on the very will of God. This systematic bias can cause you to make choices for life's second best.

Sometimes you can seek for what God knows is second best.

First Samuel 8 tells the story of Israel making a demand for a king. Twenty-five years have passed since chapter 7. God has defended Israel against the Philistines, who have had a king to lead them—a physical, visible representation who united them. Israel, on the other hand, was made up of tribes that were loosely organized. They wanted someone who would pull their tribes together and organize them so they would have a military presence in the world.

Until then, Israel did not have anybody but God to fight their battles and take care of them. Kings of other nations had lost battles, but God had never lost a battle for them. Even when it looked like they were losing, God showed up. On one occasion, the sun would have set, but the Lord said, "I am going to show you how well I can win a battle." He told the sun to stop setting, and the sun stood still (Joshua 10:12-14).

Yet Israel wanted their own king like the Philistines and the Jebusites and the Amorites. They wanted a physical representation that they could see rather than the invisible, viable presence of the mighty God. They desired to live under a monarchy rather than the theocracy He had desired for them. They were not supposed to have a human king because God alone would be their king.

But what God had provided appeared to be insufficient for the people He created. They clamored, "God, give us a king so we can be like everybody else." This is such a shame. They chose Baal, a little god that the people created, rather than God. They preferred Ashteroth, a fertility god, over the Lord Adoniah Himself.

Nevertheless, that is human nature. Because of our systemic bias, we have a preexisting condition within our souls that seems to gravitate toward second best. It does not just affect nations; individual people do the same thing even though they have received the best advice in the world.

No one is exempt from making second-best choices. John Wesley was the founder of Methodism and "saved the soul of England" according to church historians, but that still did not prevent him from seeking what would prove to be second best. Wesley had been engaged to a woman named Grace Murray, but that relationship ended in disaster. In less than three years he was ready to marry again. This woman, Mary Vazeille, was a wealthy widow who showed no interest in spiritual things. John, however, was impressed by her "industry," "exact frugality," and "uncommon neatness and cleanness." His interest in her delighted her tremendously.

But when John told Charles and his wife Sally about his intentions to marry Mary, Charles was "thunderstruck" and filled with dread. At the next church service when John announced that he would marry Mary, his brother and the congregation shook their heads in disagreement, later saying that the announcement "made [them] all hide our faces." He disregarded the counsel of his brother and sister-in-law, as well as the disapproval of his own church. In February of 1751 John Wesley and Mary were married.

The next 20 years of Wesley's life were sheer misery. At first his bride traveled with him, but his travel schedule was so relentless that this newly married 40-year-old woman was clearly hoping for something more normal. Often absent for weeks at a time, Wesley gave his wife permission to open all the mail that came for him. His mail included many letters from women seeking guidance and counsel, but Mary felt that some of them indicated more than a little affection toward her husband.

Over time Mary's jealousy increased to the point that she felt overlooked and unloved by Wesley. Not only troubled but gripped by jealousy, she traveled on his preaching circuit to spy on him. She wrote disgruntled, critical letters to him and even sent his private papers directly to his enemies so they could slander him. Eventually she publicly accused him of adultery.

On several occasions she left home, only returning after he begged her repeatedly. Their home life was very unhappy. Mary would become so embittered that she would take Wesley by his hair and drag him across the floor, pulling locks of hair from his head. Finally Mary left him for good.

All of Wesley's misery occurred because he chose unwisely against the better advice from his brother Charles and his congregation. He paid an incredible price for choosing what God knew for him was the second best.

Most of us know what it means to make a second-best choice. We may not be happy about our decision, and we surely avoid celebrating it. But if we could, as that great rhythm-and-blues theologian said, "turn back the hands of time," many of us would have bypassed those places where we stopped. We definitely would not have engaged in that behavior.

Some might say that it is just good human advice to get the counsel of many people when making big life decisions, but it is much more than that—it is biblical. In Proverbs 11:14 Solomon says that there is wisdom and safety in the counsel of many. If you do not have some *bodies* around your life whom you can talk to about the heavy issues you are confronted with at times, you need to find some people who are more spiritually mature than you are. They should be individuals who are not going to agree with everything you talk about, but rather those who would warn you not to make bad choices.

Now, the challenge of that is this: Many of us *do* have people who speak into our lives, but we refuse to listen to them. God knows that some of us have already chosen to seek out what is second best.

Wishing to be like others may cause you to ask for second best.

It is clear that the motivation of Israel was to be like other nations with a visible king. Oddly enough, they wanted to be like the Philistines and the Egyptians, nations who had been defeated and whose king had exploited the citizenry. They made a second-best choice in order to be like other nations, rather than become the distinctive people God wanted them to be. Yet, even though their rationale—"This is what other people are doing"—was natural and predictable, it was still wrong.

The motivation behind this request has to do with two things. Samuel is old now. His sons, Joel and Abijah, are egregiously immoral, living off in the margins in Beersheba. Because of their reprobate ways, they have been disqualified from being successors to the judge/

priest/prophet Samuel. Unlike his predecessor Eli, Samuel does not overlook the evil behavior and disposition of his sons. He, too, knows that they are not the ones to rule Israel. But regardless of whether they would be the judges or not, the Israelites' standing at court to make decisions with God did not give them the right to ask for what He had already denied them.

In Deuteronomy 17, God had already established that there would be a king who would arise from a particular tribe of Judah. Yet this king they were now considering hailed from the tribe of Benjamin.

That was close, but it was not right. And remember, just one degree off can send you a hundred miles in the wrong direction. With God, "close" just does not work. He is an exact God who knows what is best for you.

The Israelites demanded, "Lord, we want a king!" God replied, "Why will you not wait until I send you the king I want you to have?" The people shouted, "No! We want a king now."

Because of their incessant clamoring, God gave to them specifically what He really did not want them to have. In verse 7, He said, "They have rejected Me as king." He tells Samuel in verses 9 and 22, "Listen to them . . . . listen to them."

The Israelites would get Saul, who would fail. David, his successor, would also have his faults. Solomon had also gone in the wrong direction morally. His son Rehoboam would split the nation of Israel, and the remainder slowly disintegrated. They should have waited for God to provide the King he wanted for them. But they wanted to be like other nations, even though those people had been exploited, abused, mistreated, and marginalized.

We are always wishing to be like other people. For some reason, God is not enough for us now, and we need more than what we have already got. It is always God plus something else. Some of us go to church and wish we were somewhere else. But there are messages given to us in church that we do not hear anywhere else. Why would we swap out church for something else? We need to ask ourselves this question: What if we choose the second-best thing for ourselves?

A well-known book entitled *What If?* speculates about the positive and negatives of historical events if they had turned out differently. You can ask yourself those questions as well: What if the arrogance of Napoleon had not led him into Russia but into England instead? The consequences would have been enormous. He would have defeated England, and the whole landscape of the world would have been different. What if Hitler had gotten admitted into the fine arts school as a youngster? We could have foregone the Third Reich and escaped the Holocaust.

John F. Kennedy did not want to come to Texas, especially Dallas, that November morning in 1963. What would have happened if he had said, "I am not going"? The consequences for the world would have been greatly altered. What if Martin Luther King, Jr., when he graduated, had not gone down to Dexter, instead serving as an assistant pastor under his father? Or, what if he had taken that teaching appointment in Moorhouse or the professorial job at Boston University? What would have happened if he had accepted that pastorate in Tennessee? How would the world have looked today if he had made that second choice?

When you start making choices, you do not know what God has in store for you. Martin Luther King had no idea what his life would mean years later. Neither do you know how your life choices will affect the future of your children, grandchildren, and great-grandchildren.

How many times have lives been changed forever because we have asked for the second choice? Our marriages, businesses, education, careers, and a hundred other choices have often been made on the basis of second best.

Often God sends someone to warn us about the second-best choice.

In verse 9, God tells Samuel, "Give them what they want. They are not rejecting you; they are rejecting Me.

But warn them of what they are going to get, since they want a king like everybody else." And Samuel tells the people in verse 10, "I do not want to do it, but God told me to give you what you have been asking for. Yet I want to warn you that what you are asking for is different than what you see. All you see is the physical, visible, superficial reality of the king. You do not know what is underneath the surface. You missed that because you are just looking for a figurehead—someone who is tall and handsome and charismatic." Later, when Samuel anoints David to be the next king of Israel, God reminds him, "Man looks at the outward appearance, but God looks at the heart" (1 Samuel 16:7).

Likewise, we must stop making decisions based on how things look on the surface. Most of the mistakes we have made occur because on the surface things looked good, but underneath all that was a dangerous undertow. And God, because of His great mercy, will send somebody our way to warn us to stop.

In Yosemite Park warning signs lead to that outdoor spectacle everyone wants to see—that 317-foot waterfall into the granite basin. The view is breathtaking, and people will try to walk up there to go see it. But then they will see a guard saying, "Do not cross the line. Stay out. Do not go in. The waters look calm, but they are actually deadly." You may hear that warning, but you are so overwhelmed by the waterfall and the surrounding scenery, you no longer hear the guard say, "Do not go close to that water." There are many signs there saying, "WARNING: STOP," or "DO NOT GO IN: DEADLY WATERS." Then they have barricades with signs: "ABSOLUTELY, UNDER NO CONDITION, DO NOT ENTER." The only way you *can* enter is by climbing over the barricade. Then you have to walk 25 feet to get to the Merced River. Then there are more signs that read, "DO NOT TOUCH."

This summer, three young people in their twenties did not heed the park ranger's warnings or pay attention to the cautionary signs. Instead, they climbed over the barricade and walked 25 feet to get to the water's edge. Even though a young man who lived in the area yelled, "Do not enter!" a 21-year-old girl still stepped in the water. Immediately the undertow carried her off. Instinctively her 22-year-old friend reached out to save her, but he also was sucked under. A 27-year-old man from the group jumped into the water to rescue them, yet they all fell over the cliff to their deaths.

Some people reading about this might think that these young adults were illiterate gangsters who just did not care about those warnings. But they were actually part of a church group touring the area. In the same way, you can be heavily involved in church and still ignore dire warnings such as these. It does not matter what your title, position, or educational level might be; God is still saying no. And if God says no, it does not matter how placid, pristine, or beautiful the waters may look. God says, "That is what you see on the surface, but beneath it is an undertow that can drag you off. Do not step in that river because it can destroy your life or wreck your reputation."

In verses 10-18 Samuel clearly warns the Israelites of the consequences of asking for second best. He tells them they are setting in motion a perpetual situation of personal loss because of their choice. The earthly king would take their substance, which includes their land, children, and taxes.

The key to interpreting that passage is the word "take." They want a visible king now who is going to take from them, rather than an invisible God who keeps on giving.

What is it that you want? Personally, I do not want anything that takes life from me. Instead, I want the One who gives life to me. In John 10:10, Jesus reminded us, "The thief comes to steal, kill, and destroy, but I have come that you might have life, and have it more abundantly."

God may let you have your second choice.

The Israelites refused to listen to Samuel's warning; instead, they insisted on having a king. So God let them have what they asked for. This is a mystery beyond human comprehension.

It is difficult for believers to understand the weight and gravity of this because American Christianity has become so pragmatic. That is, to every solution there is a nut and bolt, and if it does not fit and work, then we just dismiss it. Those of us who teach and preach the Word of God are guilty of that. We have "dumbed down" God so much that people believe they can manipulate or fix Him, and the mystery of God is gone. But the moment that you think you know more than God, you have chosen second-best.

God did not want a king to rule over Israel. The prophet Samuel wanted what God desired—a theocracy, not a monarchy. In the strange reality of God's permissive will, He allowed Israel to have its way.

Leslie Weatherhead, the early 20th-century pastor of the City Temple in London, indicated three ways God's will appears to us. He has a perfect will, which is what we get if we make the first choice. He also appears to have a permissive will; this is what we get if we make the second choice. In other words, He lets us have what He does not really want us to have. His permissive will does not thwart His ultimate will, however, which *always* will be accomplished. The ultimate will cannot be compromised in any way whatsoever, regardless of whether He permits us to have certain things.

In Israel's case, God was going to have His king when He wanted His king. Even though the Hebrews had to experience the kingdoms of Saul, David, Solomon, and Rehoboam, they still did not have the ultimate king whom God wanted to reign over their lives.

Yet there was another King. In the New Testament Herod thought that he *was* that king, so he tried to murder the true King who was then just a little baby with chubby hands. He had no idea at the time that this little baby would have the power to control the celestial universe.

This picture plays out in remarkable detail in the Old Testament. In the great Exodus God had already given them the Ark of the Covenant to remind them of His viable spiritual presence. Bible scholar and former Ford executive Chuck Missler notes that when these loosely organized tribes were arranged around the tabernacle and the Ark of the Covenant, the Levites camped around the Ark. Two tribes were situated directly to the north, four tribes were positioned toward the south, three east, and three west. The tribes were arranged according to population. If a line was drawn through the camp around the Tabernacle and observed from the air, it formed a CROSS.

From the Old Testament to the New Testament, the Lord had always placed a cross over His people to remind them that there would only be one King who would truly reign over them. His name is Jesus, the King of Kings and the Lord of Lords. ✤

CHAPTER FIVE

God's Hidden Agenda

(1 Samuel 9 & 10)

"ON THE ROAD TO JERICHO" IS THE TITLE of J. Alfred Smith's memoir of racial justice, social action, and prophetic ministry. That ministry was launched on a jazz band trip from Kansas City to Oklahoma City. One night J. Alfred followed his band mates to the band shell, placed his alto saxophone to his lips, and began to play his part for "Take the A Train." What happened then was completely supernatural. On the jazz stage the presence of the divine was impressed upon his soul. There was not an audible voice like the one coming from the burning bush in front of Moses or the one present in the wind that swirled around the prophet Elijah. Yet there was something so real and unique about this voice that he had trouble keeping his mind on the song he was playing. Somewhere deep down inside, the voice of God asked, "Do you want to play one-night stands for the rest of your life?"

Before dawn the next morning, Smith rose from his bed and dressed quietly while his friends were still asleep. He grabbed his horn, walked down to the Greyhound bus station, and purchased a one-way ticket back to Kansas City, Missouri. On a bandstand with a saxophone pressed to his lips, he had started down one road; but then God about-faced his life, and he found himself on another road that led to his real destiny.

Your life can be heading in one direction, but God can arrest you and send you in another direction. First Samuel 9 and 10 tells the story of a man on one road who found himself on another road of divine purpose.

Saul lived in an outstanding home on the towering hill of Geba and enjoyed a fabulous heritage as the son of the affluent Kish. Beyond that, he was handsome and physically striking as the tallest man of his generation, which would be quite an advantage during that time for a leader. The average height in that day was hardly over five feet, so Saul stood out as the most impressive man in all of Israel. The description in verse 2 gives us our everyday phrase: he was "head and shoulders above everyone else."

One day Saul is sent out by his father to look for some lost donkeys. (A modern-day equivalent would be searching for your stolen Cadillac.) He sets off with his nameless companions, and they look for the runaway animals. After three days of fruitless searching, they end up in a little town named Zuph, where the itinerant prophet Samuel has come to hold worship services.

Saul seeks him out, thinking that he could direct them to the lost donkeys.

What happens next is beyond description. Saul's destiny is sealed after Samuel proclaims him the one anointed by God to lead Israel as their first king. At the same time Saul is on his way to Zuph looking for those lost donkeys, God has already spoken to Samuel in verses 15 and 16 of chapter 9, telling him that he would meet Saul. Young Saul goes out to find donkeys and finds his destiny instead.

Our God is a God of synchronicity who arranges events that have no obvious connection for His purposes. This entire biblical event is comparable to a farm boy from rural Britain wandering around Westminster Abbey until, all of a sudden, the Archbishop of Canterbury grabs him and crowns him the king of England.

Saul has now been presented with the gift of religious experience to add to his list. He experiences a miraculous demonstration of God's activity in his life. Saul, of course, expresses disbelief at Samuel's sudden and strange announcement. To convince the young man that he has been chosen by God to be king, Samuel tells him that he would encounter two men who would tell him where his donkeys are. After that, he would meet two men who would hand him two loaves of bread. Then, ready or not, when he returns home, young Saul would actually see two prophets descend from the high place and the Spirit of God would come upon him. Saul would join the prophets in ecstasy and praise to God. Samuel even tells Saul that God would transform his heart. Three promises are made, and three are kept. Everything that Samuel prophesies over Saul comes to pass.

This biblical story was recorded to remind us that we can be on an errand, perhaps for life, and God—without any warning or our agreement—can suddenly arrest us individually for His purposes. This is the story of most people who walk in the will of God. They were minding their own business, walking down their own street, when God arrested them and pointed them in a new direction.

God can move you and others towards His purposes and nobody knows it.

Like metal filings on a sheet of paper irresistibly attracted by a magnet, Saul, coming from one direction, and Samuel, arriving from the other, are headed to a human-divine encounter that would alter the future of the world forever. Samuel, the circuit rider priest/prophet/judge, has traveled to this small village because no national shrine exists anymore to hold religious services. Only makeshift papier-maché places like this one are peppered throughout the region. At the same time, coming from the hill country is this tall, handsome Saul, looking for donkeys. Above it all, God has placed them on a collision course to remind them that when they come together, His purposes would override their intentions.

Similar stories such as that abound throughout the annals of Christendom.

- Gardner C. Taylor despised preachers, even though his father was one, and considered the pastoral ministry a second-rate vocation. In fact, he had already decided to go to law school in Michigan. One night in rural Louisiana, while chauffeuring the president of Leland College, he was involved in an accident. He thought his destiny was sealed—in jail. But at the inquest worthy of a "Perry Mason" TV drama, two unknown witnesses exonerated him. At that unlikely moment, he received the call to preach. Recently *TIME* named him the "dean of American preachers."

- Billy Graham was an awkward, gangly North Carolina dairy farmer's son who attended a tent revival being held by an eccentric traveling evangelist named Mordecai Hamm. Under that tent he was converted to Christianity. It was a divine appointment that changed the course of history.

- Eight-year-old Rebekah Ann Naylor was listening to her own father Robert E. Naylor, pastor of First Baptist Church in Columbia, South Carolina, preach. She walked down the aisle and told her father that she would be a missionary surgeon. Years later she became a legend in Bangalore, India, after building hospitals, nursing schools, and other works for Jesus—all because of a divine collision that occurred on a Sunday morning.

- B.H. Carroll, the longtime elderly pastor of First Baptist Church in Waco, Texas, was on a train ride in the Panhandle. God spoke to him right then to start a seminary in Texas. People thought he had lost his mind when he stood up on that train and said, "I'll do it!" Carroll went on to found the largest theological seminary in North America, which would train more foreign missionaries than any Protestant seminary in history.

God has remarkable ways of arranging things. It does not matter whether you are a college student in a car wreck, a teenager in a tent revival, an eight-year-old girl in a church service, or an old man on a train. God can put you on a new road to destiny.

The American poet Robert Frost echoed this principle for all time in his famous 1920 work, "The Road Not Taken."

Two roads diverged in a yellow wood,
And sorry I could not travel both
And be one traveler, long I stood
And looked down one as far as I could
To where it bent in the undergrowth;

Then took the other, as just as fair,
And having perhaps the better claim
Because it was grassy and wanted wear,
Though as for that the passing there
Had worn them really about the same,

And both that morning equally lay
In leaves no step had trodden black.
Oh, I marked the first for another day!
Yet knowing how way leads on to way
I doubted if I should ever come back.

I shall be telling this with a sigh
Somewhere ages and ages hence:
Two roads diverged in a wood, and I,
I took the one less traveled by,
And that has made all the difference.

You may find yourself without resources and success, but God can meet you at that very moment.

Samuel and Saul have come from opposite directions to meet at a strange place called Zuph. They do not know at the time that they are on a divine collision course where they would encounter God's purposes. Notice that God does not do this in the mountains of Ephraim or the hill country of Ramah. He does it at Zuph.

Zuph is not so much a point on the map as it is a situation in life. Things are tough at Zuph. There is never enough at Zuph. At this place, we have lost what we were looking for; it is gone and we are out of resources. Zuph is a place where we all find ourselves at some time in life, chasing something that we cannot find and using up all the resources of life doing it.

Saul and his men have run out of resources at Zuph. When they count their money, they realize they have insufficient funds to buy the customary gift for Samuel. They have experienced what businesspersons call "lost opportunity cost." (This means that if you pursue one thing, you cannot pursue another.) They have lost all opportunity pursuing what they could not find. Here they are, in a hard place, but just at the right time, God intervenes.

When all seems lost, God's perfect timing sets the stage for a future greater than you can imagine.

Realizing that the search for the donkeys is beyond their reach because they are out of resources, Saul decides to go home. But his men believe that he might be quitting too soon because there is a man of God in town who might be able to help them. At just the right time, the circuit rider prophet Samuel has come to Zuph to hold church services.

Some of you may be ready to quit too soon. Perhaps the circumstances are just not quite working out the way you thought they would. You may have every reason to quit because you feel like you have gone as far as you could. But you may not want to quit until you hear what the man of God has to say. It is no accident that this nameless companion tells Saul to find out what Samuel says. Samuel is respected throughout the land because what he prophesies comes to pass.

If you do not have that particular person in your life yet, you need to find him because the time will come when you are in Zuph—and it is tough and rough. You need someone who can handle your particular situation, and God will give you one of His men to help you with it. When you are in a tight spot, you need someone to point you in the right direction. Sometimes God will put you on a road to see if you are paying attention to the message He has got waiting for you so you can get where you think you are supposed to go.

God has been trying to change the direction for you, yet you are nervous and scared. You have been talking to everyone but the right people. They are saying, "They are offering you a lot of money there, so you should take that job." But sometimes what God is offering you is not a matter of dollars and cents or material things. At any rate, God will lead you if you are willing to be led. He will be there for you at the right time and place.

God may do something great in your life privately before He does it publicly.

God has already made secret announcements to both Samuel and Saul before He tells the nation that Saul will be the first king. In verse 20 of chapter 9 Samuel gives him this individual promise in private. Then Saul is anointed twice—once with some of the people in private at the banquet (10:1), followed by the anointing before all of the people in public (v. 24).

Sometimes God has to do what He does in your life privately before He will do it publicly. The mistake that some of us have made is that we have gone public too soon. While God is still working the details out, we must let Him do it. After He does, then we can go public with it.

When Samuel and Saul meet, Saul looks up and asks him where he can find the prophet. Samuel replies, "I am he. I know who you are. God sent you chasing donkeys in order to find your destiny and go to your dynasty." Samuel then tells Saul what his future looks like.

For the second anointing Samuel invites Saul to dinner in the company of 30 people to provide accountability. To make sure that he is truly speaking for the Lord, Samuel sees to it that integrity is locked up in this situation.

In verse 22 of chapter 10, Saul tries to hide from everyone by burying himself in a garbage can. Samuel tells him to get out of the garbage because he knows that is not where Saul is supposed to be. God does not intend for him to grovel in the dirt; instead, He wants to raise him up to receive the kingly diadem.

God can anoint your life in multiple places, and whatever He says *will* come to pass. But God often gives you the revelation privately before He does it publicly. That is why, in the Sermon on the Mount, Jesus uses the expression, "Do not cast your pearls before swine." Some people do not deserve to hear what God is doing in your life. Everything God does is not meant for you to talk about, but to meditate on. When God shows you the right time, then you can talk about it. He may be acting in such a way in your life that it would be premature to tell anybody what is going on.

Pastor Rick Warren received a message as a boy preacher from W. A. Criswell, who was, at that time, pastor of First Baptist Church of Dallas. After Criswell shook his hand, he told him, "God has something special for you and your future." Rick Warren never discussed that word with anyone for 30 years. After Criswell died and Warren was older and more spiritually mature, then he talked about it.

On the other hand, some of you have shrugged off what God has told you. You fail to give much attention to those individuals God has put in your life, such as pastors, Sunday school teachers, or grandparents. These wise persons have tried to counsel and encourage you with words like, "There is a reason this is not working for you. You were not made for this." But you refuse to listen and go down the road you want to anyway. Soon, however, you discover that God is saying, "Wait a minute. You should listen to these people. I put them there for a specific purpose." You soon find yourself getting into trouble simply because you have chosen to ignore the advice of those to whom you are accountable.

When are you going to trust God to let Him enable you to do what He has called you to do? You do not have to be a preacher or missionary to do what God has called you to do. But whatever God has called you to do, do it!

When God calls you to do something, He will give you sufficient encouragement to vindicate His purpose.

Samuel has given all of these messages to Saul, but at this time, Saul just cannot believe it. He reminds Samuel that he has come from a little tribe in a little place. Essentially he is asking Samuel, "How can God use me?"

Many of you may be asking the same question: How can God use me, with my background and sinful history? Yet God can give you sufficient encouragement in the time of need to vindicate His purpose.

Samuel gives Saul three promises to confirm God's choice of him as king. First, Saul would meet two people at Rachel's well who would tell him that his donkeys are found. After this sign comes to pass, Saul learns a valuable lesson: *God will return to you what you have lost.*

Some of you may have lost the joy of your salvation because you just cannot run on empty. You have to fill the empty place, but you have discovered that you cannot fill it with the wrong things. Instead, your joy is meant to be fueled by the Word of God and the Holy Spirit. Only those two elements can fill you and give you the joy you used to have. In other words, you cannot just eat for 30 minutes on Sunday and think that will keep you fully nourished spiritually until the next Sunday.

Samuel then tells Saul that he would meet another group of people at Tabor who would give him bread, lambs, and wine. Saul does indeed find these people, and they feed him. The second lesson is this: *God will give you physical provision to sustain you on life's journeys.*

Do you have faith to trust God to provide for whatever you need when you require it? It is not up to you to know how He will provide for you, either. Some of you have been begging for God to feed and fuel and fix you; but when the Lord sends His provision to you in strange and unexpected ways, you refuse His help. Yet you need to be content in knowing that whatever way God sends His provision, that is how you will be supplied.

Samuel then tells Saul that on his way back, upon encountering some prophets prophesying and praising God, he would start prophesying and praising too. That would be a sign that God's anointing is with him. This is the last lesson: *God will give you spiritual renewal to continue your journey.*

On your journey of life, remember that God will give you strength when you are weak. God will renew you so that your feet will run and your hands will clap, even when you do not feel like it. That is why He will do it— because your faith is not based on the way you feel. Faith and feelings are two different things. You do not worship the Lord just because you feel good. Sometimes you worship just because you have to. The mind works on two levels—the emotional and the rational. The emotional level always wants to feel good, while the rational level rarely operates that way.

I read that some scientists put together a special alarm clock to get people out of bed. It was designed to roll off the nightstand and into the hall, forcing the sleeper to wake up and chase after it. But behavioral psychologists said that the device would soon lose its effectiveness because eventually the "feeling good" aspect of sleep would override the "making sense" aspect.

But if you can get the "makes sense" aspect to fit in with feeling good, that is when you become a whole person. Some of you, for example, are constantly striving to diet and exercise to lose weight. You often do not follow through with your regimen because you "do not feel like it." Similarly, many of you say, "I know I need to go to church (or pray), but I do not feel like it." But you have to get to the point where you simply put those feelings aside and just do it. You will soon discover that when you just do it, then you will feel like it.

You can be on one road, heading in one direction, but when God puts you on another road, you will be traveling in a completely different direction. You need to let God do this so you can achieve your destiny in Him. ✤

CHAPTER SIX

A Good Look in the Rear-view Mirror

(1 Samuel 12)

SOMETIMES PEOPLE GO BACKWARDS in order to go forwards. That is the case of people who have engaged in a sports phenomenon called "backwards running." These individuals believe that they can advance by going backwards. Wikipedia has given some depth to the definition of backwards running by calling it "retro running" or "retro locomotion." A 42-year-old Filipino, Jojo Bigay, made it his goal to break the double Guinness world record held by a Ghanan and a German. Ferdie Ato Adoboe from Ghana had set the previous world record for the 100-meter with a time of 13.6 seconds back in 1994. In 2007, Roland Wegner from Germany equaled that record. In a practice run, Adoboe's and Wegner's records were broken by Bigay, who recorded a time of 13.2 seconds.

On the other hand, there are those who look at things backwards in a phenomenological way in different fields. The world-class pianist and musical prodigy Franz Lizst could play music upside down and backwards, or from right to left. Audiences were constantly amazed at his ability to do things backwards.

There is something fascinating about looking back at our lives, which is what valedictory speeches really are. Young people compete academically to achieve the highest grade point average so they can say that they are the valedictorians of their high schools. They do not just give future projections, but they also review where they have come from.

Farewell speeches are like that. One of the most famous in American history took place in the middle of the 20th century at Mason Temple Church of God in Christ in Memphis, Tennessee, during the Poor Man's March. Martin Luther King, Jr. was feverish and sick. He should have stayed in bed, but his friends urged him to come. He had not written out his speech, so he spoke extemporaneously—out of his overflow. He said, "I have been to the mountaintop. And I may not get there with you, but we as a people shall get to the Promised Land." People heard him that night, and those words indeed became a farewell valedictory. Today, we know that much of his words have come to pass.

And who can forget that day in military history when Douglas MacArthur went to his alma mater and stood before those promising young cadets at West Point? He looked out over the audience and said these words: "Old soldiers never die; they just fade away. My last conscious thought shall be, 'The Corps, the Corps, the Corps.' "

Whether you stand on one side of politics or the other, who was more prophetic about the military than Eisenhower? At the end of his life, he predicted that the military-industrial complex would be the dominant force in the world. We have lived to see that.

You can tell people, "Either things are right or I will make them right."

But Samuel's farewell address was different from those given by these famous men. He does something that no one else does. Samuel is interested in the people whom he has served. He is able to check vital items off the list of his reputation. He asks them, "Have I done what I said I would do?" And here he looks in the rear-view mirror and simply says to a people who have observed his life over the years, "Either it is right, or I will make it right."

Even though we may work out in the gym and eat right, the truth of the matter is that each one of us is going to die. One of the failures of American Christianity is that we talk about living, but we fail to discuss dying. The great Christians of the past spoke equally about life and death. Cars and clothes and cash are nice to have, but there is one place where they do not make any impression at all. This is where Samuel is standing—looking at the rear-view mirror.

When you are looking in your own rear-view mirror, make sure what you say stands the test of time. In verses 2 and 12 of the 12th chapter, Samuel draws our attention to the primary purpose of his valedictory speech, and that is this: "You have received what you have been asking for. You wanted to be like other nations. You are God's covenant people, and you had what no other nation could boast of. The invisible reality of God led you from the beginning until now. You looked and you wanted to imitate what you saw the Philistines and the Ammonites doing. And now God is giving to you what He really did not want you to have. Now that you have it, here are my words to you: Live obediently according to what you have signed your contract to, and God will continue to bless you by feeding your crops and livestock and extending your land. But if you do not, woe unto you. Mourning will come to you."

This is not an "I told you so" speech from Samuel. He is merely saying, "You got what you asked for. Now live up to what you asked for." This is the question you and I have got to ask ourselves, the one that all conscientious people ask themselves: *When I lay my head down on its final pillow, when the shadow gathers cold and long at the end of my bed, when family and friends gather around me as I have one foot in time and the other in eternity, will the words I have spoken stand the test of time?* That is the reality of life.

I have stood at hundreds of gravesides and preached many funeral sermons. Sometimes people have come up to me afterward and complimented me on the message. I tell them that it is easy to do that when people have actually lived out the sermon I was preaching.

For other funeral sermons, I have had to dig deep to say something positive. Typically I would select a text and exegete it. When you come to the end of your life, you do not want your pastor to just find a Bible text and do a hermeneutical interpretation. Instead, you should want your life to be an illustration of the text he preaches.

When Martin Luther turned the world upside down in the Reformation, the Roman Catholic Church excommunicated him. He came to that moment all of us come to—when we stand on the edge of eternity to stare at God face to face. Someone came to him and said, "Herr Martin, can you die by the words that you lived?" He answered with one word, "Ja."

That ought to be the same with us. Even though we are not quite the people we want to be, we can still die with a good conscience, knowing that we have tried to live what we have talked about, instead of being hypocrites.

Such was the case with Samuel, who has led the nation of Israel with spiritual integrity. And now, he is speaking to a group of people who has literally fallen into hypocrisy.

You do not want to talk about God in church and live like you do not know Him out in the world. You need to live for Him out there, where no one is looking at you. That character trait is called integrity.

This farewell speech of Samuel's, beginning in verse 3, poses a thought-provoking question for us to consider: When we gaze in the rear-view mirror of life, will our lives pass the integrity test?

In verse 3, Samuel asks the Israelites, "Whose ox have I stolen? Whose donkey have I taken? Who have I bribed or extorted? If that person is here and can name the occasion when I have done so, I will make it right." In biblical times, oxen and donkeys were the basic means of transportation, so this is a crucial question for Samuel to ask.

There are some deeds you have done that you can never make right. The nursery rhyme is true: "Humpty Dumpty sat on a wall/Humpty Dumpty had a great fall/All of the King's horses and all of the King's men/ Couldn't put Humpty back together again." When certain things are broken, the most educated and wealthiest people cannot put them back together again.

It is hard for us to accept that grim reality because contemporary Christianity teaches us that we can do whatever we want to do and then fix it later. But that is an outright lie. There are some consequences of our deeds that we must live with for the rest of our lives. But if, by God's grace, there is something broken that we *can* fix, we ought to go and fix it as soon as we can.

If you stole an object from someone, for example, you can make that right by giving it back. If you slandered someone by castigating their character, you can stop talking negatively about them and start telling the truth. If you have received a gift from someone and you are too stubborn to say thanks, you can contact that person and ask them to forgive you for your ingratitude. This is called making restitution, which is the promise Samuel made: "If it is not right, then I will make it right."

Restitution—giving back, or making right—is the heart of Christianity. Some Christians believe that they have never done anything that deserves either contrition (crying over things that cannot be made right) or restitution (making things right). Yet this is merely superficial Christianity that does not make any impression on our culture.

In Luke 19, little Zaccheus had been working on the inside with the Roman government, taxing his own countrymen. He was viewed as marginal and out of bounds. Nobody liked him. The only reason they put up with him was because he had money. Upon hearing that

Jesus was coming to town, he closed his tax office and went to see Him and His parade of followers. Unable to see, Zaccheus climbed up a sycamore tree. But he did not know that he would soon be getting an eyeful of who Jesus really was.

In verse 5 Jesus said, "Zaccheus, come down, for today I must stay at your house." What He was actually saying was, "Salvation and deliverance is coming to your house." Of all the people He could have stayed with, He chose the worst scoundrel in town. When He got to the house, salvation also got there. Jesus did not preach to him, urging him to give back and do right. All He did was show up at his house. In verse 8 Zaccheus said, "My Lord, I have extorted my brothers and mistreated them, so I am going to return four times what I have stolen." In the same way, when the Lord has brought salvation into your house, you ought to make restitution with somebody.

In 2011 Plano teenager Ashley Donaldson found an envelope with $2,000 in it. She did not know whom it belonged to, but she knew it was not hers, so she took it to the police station. After she turned the money in, a man wrote a letter to her, expressing his disbelief that a teenager would return such a large sum of money. He enclosed a check to her for $2,000. Another lady heard about this and sent Ashley a check for $4,000. Others also gave her money, indicating that they hoped the financial gifts would help pay for her college education.

Something good always happens when you do something you know is right. Josh Farren, a struggling Utah artist, and his wife finally moved into their dream house. One couple was moving out, so they moved in. One day when he went into his man-cave and started cleaning up, he stumbled upon some bags that held an approximate total of $45,000. He told his wife and friends that he needed to contact the former owners and return their money to them. His friends disagreed with him, claiming that the bags of money came with the house. Josh told them that giving the money back would teach his two sons what integrity really looks like. He called the previous owners, who did not even realize the money was missing. However, they still needed it because they were an older couple who had been saving for years.

What you say comes to pass.

In chapter 10, Israel got what they wanted—a king—but they also got a drought. In verse 16 of chapter 12, the drought ends after Samuel said the rain would come. That is God's way of saying that what He promises will always comes true. In verse 22, Samuel reminds the people that the Lord promised He would never abandon them—and He never did. God has made promises, and He always keeps them.

Even though you are not Samuel, you can still learn a huge lesson from him: If you make a promise, it should be one that you keep. Samuel lived long enough for his words to be vindicated. Will the words that you say stand the test of time when you have reached the end of your life?

Some secular and religious prophets have become a joke throughout the world because what they predicted did not come to pass. In the sixties, famed astrologers like Jeanne Dixon made some predictions about the future that just did not happen. Recently Bishop Harold Camping, the elderly radio preacher from California, twice predicted that the end of the world would happen—once in May of 2011, and then again in October of the same year. He is now a living joke.

You must make sure that this does not happen to you. As Jesus exhorted His disciples in the Sermon on the Mount, "Let your yea be yea and your nay be nay." Just a short time ago, crucial business transactions were conducted on the basis of a handshake because a man's word was his bond. This is a vital question to consider: How much is your word (promise) worth?

In the New Testament, Jesus made an eternal promise in John 14:1-3 that is often mentioned during funeral sermons: "Let not your heart be troubled. You believe in God; believe also in Me. In My Father's house are many mansions. If it were not so, I would have told you. I go to prepare a place for you. And if I go, I shall come again to receive you unto Myself." When they asked Him how they would know the way, the Lord answered, "I am the way, the truth, and the life. No man comes to the Father but by Me."

In verse 16, Jesus added, "When I go, I am not going to leave you by yourself. I am going to give you the Paraclete, the Comforter. He will be a Helper to you. When you are lost, He will find you. When you need to be taught, He will teach you. When you need guidance, He will lead you. I have to go away so the Holy Spirit can come." And after Jesus died, was buried, and rose again, the Holy Spirit did indeed fall upon the disciples at Pentecost through the wind and fire.

Unless Jesus comes to get us when He comes again, we are all going to have a eulogy. But the real eulogy will be the one we have already delivered by the unspoken way we have lived our own individual lives. ❖

CHAPTER SEVEN

Know When to Hold 'Em, Know When to Fold 'Em

(1 Samuel 16:1-13)

MOST OF US CHUCKLE OVER THE WORDS of this chapter title because we know the story behind those words in the song "The Gambler." A younger poker player is on a train ride to his poker-playing destination. According to the lyrics, he is accompanied by an old poker player who is able to read faces. He says to the young, distraught poker player that he would give him the key to his success if he gave him a drink of his whiskey and a cigarette in return. While drinking and smoking, this older poker player begins to share his insights on reading faces and playing the game. Then he comes to the central idea of what he wants this young man to know, and it is simply this: "You have to know when to hold 'em, know when to fold 'em/Know when to walk away, know when to run."

This is a great revelation because those who play the game, whether it is poker, spades, whist, or blackjack, know that this is just common card-playing philosophical sense. There comes a time when "you have to hold 'em," and then there are other times when "you have to fold 'em." You have to walk away from some tables, and from others you just have to run.

As long as those words just hang around poker tables, they pose no real problem. In fact, to most of us they are superficial and sometimes silly. To people who gamble for a living, however, they are very serious words. Yet when you move that game of trying to read people's faces from the poker table to the table of life, those words take on an entirely different gravitas of meaning. Sometimes you just have to know when to walk away from people, groups, and programs when God says it is time to fold 'em.

When you do not know when to fold 'em, God might repent that He even put you in position.

You can go with God's program even when it contradicts what you want. Samuel finds himself at that place. He had never wanted a king for the nation of Israel. He enjoyed God being the sovereign ruler of the nation, but he had to submit to God's acceptance of Israel's request. They ended up getting their king.

On several occasions, King Saul did not do what God commanded him to do. God, for example, had an extermination/termination program He wanted Saul to engage in. In short, He wanted him to wipe out all the enemies of Israel. Saul took it upon himself to do just that, with the exception of the better spoils of battle, which he kept for himself. He rationalized this move by thinking, *God could not have meant exactly what He said.* So he felt like he needed to help God by giving the command his own interpretation. To Saul, God meant for him to exterminate the enemy nation, but not their king Agag, and certainly not the choicest livestock—the best sheep and goats. So he kept them.

At that moment, God sent Samuel to tell Saul, "Why did you play that hand?" It had already been dealt, and God just said, "It is time to fold 'em." But Saul kept playing, thinking, *Surely God did not mean for me to eliminate the king. To have a king in our custody gives us some leverage with military strategy. This increases our collection, and we need sacrifices as well. After all, why would God want us to get rid of the sheep and goats? He did not mean that. Surely He wanted me to interpret that command for Him.* God told Samuel, "See what I am working with? He does not know when to hold 'em, or when to fold 'em."

Verse 11 of chapter 15 says that God rejected the king and now Samuel is grieved. He is grieved to the point of being inconsolable, as if a loved one has died. There are not enough tissues to wipe away his tears. He discovered that sometimes you have to walk away, even when you have done exactly what God has told you to do.

In verse 23 of chapter 15, God says to Samuel,

"Remind him that he rejected My word—the same word that established him as king. By rejecting that word, he has rejected Me. It is time now for him to fold 'em.'"

Knowing when to hold 'em or fold 'em means hearing the voice of God clearly.

Previously in the third chapter, Samuel was repeatedly called by God in the early morning hours. Samuel responded by going to Eli and saying, "Here I am." But Eli told him that it was the Lord who was calling him. The next time God called Samuel, he answered, "Speak, Lord. Your servant is listening."

Now Samuel has comes to another time in his life when he must hear God's voice clearly. He says to himself, *Not only do I have to hear Him, but I have to do what He says.*

There are times in life when the word of God comes to you, and you have to ask Him, "Lord, help me to be sensitive enough to hear what You are saying." You are an energetic, alive, responsive human being. Ask God to help you open your ears so you can distinguish what He is saying, when He is saying it, and how to do what He is telling you to do. That is one of the greatest lessons you can learn in life—to distinguish the voice of God.

I have often heard people in church ask, "How do you know the difference between the voice of God and

Satan?" If you are unable to make that distinction, you are not a Christian. It does not take a Rhodes scholar to distinguish between the voice of God and the voice of the Enemy—the voice of ultimate life versus the voice of ultimate destruction. As Christians, we must be able to listen to the voice of God.

It is time to fold 'em when you cannot rehabilitate what God will not resuscitate.

For some reason, the church does not understand this concept. When you engage your life with people, it does not matter if you are anointed, licensed, and ordained—they will disappoint you. And the big disappointment for Samuel is that Saul became Samuel's project when Saul was no longer God's project. He was trying to rehabilitate that which God told Samuel, "I have no rehabilitation for him. I dealt him his hand, and he played instead of folding when I told him to do so. He did not close when he should have. Away with him!"

It sounds harsh, but there comes a time when you just have to move away from people, groups, and programs. That is just a hard reality. There are some people right now in your life you are trying to help, but you feel like you are their rehabilitation. You have tried everything, and you end up feeling like you are their Messiah or Jesus. If they are going to get saved, you feel like you are going to be the one to bring them to that place. However, the Lord has told you that because these people are toxic and poisonous, you need to fold 'em and walk away.

There are also groups—organizations, fraternities, sororities, clubs, institutions, and some churches—who refuse to be rehabilitated. God has tried everything He can do with them and given them every opportunity to change. As Christians we cannot take God's grace for granted just because we have put up brick and mortar on the church buildings. If our churches walk away from the will of God, all we will have to show for our efforts are big buildings with many empty people sitting inside of them.

Sometimes we have to walk away from not just individuals or groups, but also programs that are no longer working. Some people get very upset because their churches decide not to use the same programs they have in the past. For them, it is as if God no longer has any creativity, ingenuity, or foresight to offer them. When some programs come to a natural end, we just need to write "Rest in Peace" over them and let God birth a new idea in our imaginations. There are some new things that God wants to do. This does not mean that what we did was not productive. It just means that the program is no longer what God desires for the church. And God wants to do something new inside of each one of us—a new praise, a new prayer, a new sermon, or a new song. We should not be afraid to do what is new and improved in the Lord's eyes.

We stand at the best time of our lives as the church, as a city, as a state, and as a country. Yet some of us in the church do not want to release those programs we have been using because we have enjoyed such great success with them in the past. Like old clothes we used to wear, the only time we really think about them is when we are digging them out. We just refuse to throw them out or give them away. As Christians following the Lord, however, we must discern His will regarding certain people, groups, and programs. In other words, we have to know when to hold 'em and when to fold 'em, when to walk away and when to run.

We can know when to hold 'em or fold 'em because God has prearranged our lives.

Sometimes we must let God deal us a brand new hand of cards. One of the reasons for doing this involves God's prearrangements in our lives. We can trust God because He is always working ahead of us. One of the tragedies of contemporary Christianity is our obsessive need to understand everything about God. By doing this, however, we erase the mystery of His providence. I am not saying that we cannot know God, but we must understand that it is impossible to manage God and understand all His mysteries. Worldly logic and pragmatism says that if you cannot add one plus one plus one and get three, then it cannot be. But as Christians we know that it all depends on who is counting. Foundational to the Christian faith is the doctrine that says God the Father plus God the Son plus God the Holy Spirit equals one. And it does not matter if you do not understand it completely or not. All you have to know is that God, Jesus, and the Holy Spirit are operative right now.

It is indeed a mystery, but it is a mystery that you can embrace because God is a moving, dynamic God. The abolitionist's hymn entitled "The Battle Hymn of the Republic" has six stanzas that all end the same way: "His truth is marching on." God is moving, arranging, and fixing situations. We have a God who is not static, still, stationary, or living in the past. He is a present help right now.

Perhaps you have difficulty embracing that concept. Many of you have found yourselves in places where you never calculated that you would be. Some of you are in good places, others in bad ones, yet you still know in your heart that you are in the will of God. You study your Bible and pray. You have trusted God and depended upon Him. Those of you who have come out on the other side of a dark place by God's deliverance may not have understood what was happening when you were going through the process. At any rate, God has allowed you to experience these difficult trials so you could help those who are going through similar circumstances now. If you are in the will of God, even if it was a bad place, now that you have come out of it, it serves as a life lesson that the God who leads you in can also lead you out.

This is part of the mystery of God's divine prearrangement. We only need to read a couple of Old Testament stories to know that is true. Abraham was commanded by God to offer up his only son Isaac as a sacrifice on Mount Moriah. When they got there, Abraham tied up his son and placed him on the altar. He drew the blade and lifted it up, and when he was ready to take his son's life, he heard God say, "Stay your hand." Abraham looked to the right and saw a ram caught in the thicket. He did not know that would happen when he woke up that morning, but before he got back home, he was able to say, "The Lord surely does know how to provide."

God's prearrangement can also be found in the story of Moses. After his birth, his mother protected him as long as she could from being slaughtered as a result of the Pharaoh's edict. When she could not nurse the baby Moses any longer, she placed him in a basket and pushed him down the Nile River. At just the right moment, the

Pharaoh's daughter stepped into the river to bathe and espied the basket. They would not have paid any attention to it, but the baby Moses began to cry at just the right time. She drew him out of the water, which is how he got his name.

Moses did not know that he would be raised in Pharaoh's house, adopted by Pharaoh as his son, and educated at the university as an architect, mathematician, and statesman. God had to bring it all back to his remembrance when He was 80. He asked Moses, "Do you think you spent 40 years in Egypt for no reason? I prearranged it all because there were certain things you had to know about Egypt if you were going to say, 'Let My people go!' "

Some of you have been placed in specific situations by God's hand, but you think you are there by accident. Yet the Lord has already prearranged your circumstances so that everything will come out all right (Romans 8:28).

In the first part of chapter 16 God sends Samuel to Bethlehem to Jesse's house. Samuel is traveling there discreetly so that Saul would not suspect that he was plotting a coup to overthrow the kingdom. In verse 4 the elders of the town ask Samuel, "Do you come peaceably?" This question teaches us that sometimes we ought to tremble when God's man comes into our midst. There once was a time when God's holy and anointed person showed up, everyone knew that someone with His authority had just walked into the room.

Recently, certain church movements have stripped away the mystery of ministry in the guise of wanting to be like everyone else. Church growth specialists advised congregations that they could not increase their membership by using words like "sin" and "righteousness" because the religious sensibilities of people would be offended. And then modern preachers, desiring to be accepted and liked, started preaching "nice," palatable sermons. Now they have just become bland, insipid, placid, banal preachers who do not threaten anyone. No one worries when they show up, and no one pays any attention when they say anything because they talk just like everyone else.

Modern-day preachers choose not to use church language anymore because they think people will not understand it. Yet the church is the only place that abandons its vocabulary. Other fields such as technology, politics, and sociology do not do this. The church's language has been so watered down that people who attend services do not even realize they have been to church. They probably will not hear about God, and if they do, they will hear preachers telling them that He is always trying to give them something. These pastors will assure their congregations that Jesus is just their partner and friend, and the Holy Spirit is just someone who will make them feel good.

It is time for God to raise up holy, anointed men and women who are not trying to get another car or house or more wealth but rather standing up and causing us to tremble. There ought to be some trembling when pastors address racism and sexism and militarism and ageism. When an anointed man or woman of God stands up to preach, the people ought to know that he or she is bringing a message straight from heaven.

Your future may be different and not look at all like what you expect. Samuel goes down to Jesse's house to anoint the next king of Israel. When Samuel arrives, everyone is nervous because the judge/priest/prophet of God is there. The townspeople are hoping that he has not come to stir up any problems. Samuel reassures them by saying that he is there on official business. He asks Jesse if he can see his eight sons, so Jesse brings them in—one by one.

Samuel has this proclivity to choose based on externals. When Eliab, Jesse's eldest son, enters, Samuel is impressed by his physical looks and winsomeness. He feels that Eliab would make a good king, but God rejects him. He intervenes before Samuel looks at another son of Jesse's by telling him not to look at outward appearances because He looks on the heart instead. Jesse presents each one of his sons to Samuel, but God turns them all down. Samuel asks him if he has any more sons, and Jesse reluctantly admits that he has another one, but he is unusual because he is always out there in the field with the sheep. Jesse believes that all David will ever be is a shepherd. Samuel insists on seeing him. David walks in, and even though he is not the best-looking son, God chooses him—the one everyone else has overlooked.

God can make your future different in very unlikely ways. He can do whatever He wants to do with whomever He chooses. He does not require a person to have a certain IQ or elite background before He can use him or her. That is not the way He does things. He reaches down in the strangest places.

In another Bethlehem many centuries later, God sent His hope to the world in the form of His Son, Jesus Christ. Some people thought He should have been born in Rome so He could have come from the political lineage of the Caesars. That would have given Him the political power to execute His judgment upon the earth. But God said no. Some others thought He should have come by way of the intelligentsia in Athens. He could have been born in the home of a scholar like Socrates or Plato, but God said no. Since He would be a religious leader, some people thought He should have been born in Jerusalem. He could have come through the house of

Caiaphas or Annas and been part of the religious establishment. Again, God said no. Where would Jesus come from then? He would be born in a little town called Bethlehem and grow up in the ghettos of Nazareth.

God can do exceedingly above and beyond what we can ever ask or think (Ephesians 3:20). Just know that there are times when you have got to hold 'em and when to fold 'em. When you walk away, remember that God never told you to leave something just to find yourself later in the same kind of situation. Whatever you walk away from, God has always got something better for you to walk into. ✤

Salvator Rosa (Italian, 1615 – 1673)
Apparition of the Spirit of Samuel to Saul, 1668
Musée du Louvre (Paris, France)

CHAPTER EIGHT

Bewitched: A Cameo Appearance

(1 Samuel 28:3-19)

SAMUEL'S NAME HAD BEEN ANNOUNCED at the beginning of the book by God when he was just a little boy (3:2), and now in the afterlife his name has been announced by this sorceress who has called him forward from the grave. The first announcement of Samuel's name at the shrine has settled the matter of his vocation. In the afterlife, because he has been called from the bosom of Abraham, his reputation is settled. His entire life has consistently reflected authentic character. He has been faithful and trustworthy to God.

The message of this chapter does not imply that when you need help, you should seek out a spiritualist or a soothsayer—somebody who can carry on a séance to call somebody back from the grave. The church completely rejects trafficking with mediums and spirits, which includes the use of Ouija boards, astrology, Tarot cards, crystal balls, and palm reading. Christians have to continue standing against the practice because right now in America, 1-900-PSYCHIC-FRIEND is a multi-billion dollar industry. Somebody is always trying to get in contact with somebody beyond somewhere.

One reason the church does not engage in these practices is that no one has ever returned from the grave and said anything. We build our faith on what the Bible says. There have been those who have come back from the dead; they are just not saying anything. During the ministry of the prophet Elijah, the widow's son was brought back from the dead, but he did not say anything. The son of the widow in Nain who was raised from the dead by Jesus said nothing. Jairus' daughter was also brought back from the dead, but she did not say anything either. They held a banquet for Lazarus, but he did not mention anything about his death experience.

When Samuel came back from the dead, he did say something, but it was not good news. The moral of the story is this: if you bring somebody back from the dead, be prepared to receive some bad news. But there is another side of this story that you *can* see: You can live your life so that you are remembered with reverence as one who offered wisdom, counsel, hope, and power.

Live so that when great challenges come their way, they wish you were back.

If Saul had been our principal character, the story would be completely different. Instead Samuel, even though he is dead, has the main role in this chapter.

The more we read in the Scriptures about the impact of this prophet's life, the harder it is to believe that he is no longer on the scene. But Samuel now is dead. This story was recorded in the Bible to remind us that we can live our lives in the face of crises with such wisdom and faith that when people are confronted with their own challenges of life, they wish we were back to advise them.

In chapter 28, Saul is once again embroiled in conflict with the Philistines. The Israelites are separated from their enemy's camp at Shunem by the valley of Gilboa. The story says that the heart of Saul has been stricken with terror and fear. The last time he went head to head with the Philistines in chapter 7, he had access to the counsel of Samuel, who told him just what to do. We are not told in later chapters what Saul has been doing; but whatever it is, he certainly has not been putting much emphasis in the development of his army. They are weak, tired, out of shape, and spent. Now that it is time to go into battle, they are not prepared, so Saul is frightened. Samuel is dead and gone, and he desperately needs advice on how to proceed.

According to verses 4 through 6, Saul tried calling on God, but He refused to listen to him. God would not even answer him in the three Old Testament ways that He was accustomed to answer. God would not answer Saul through a dream; he did not even have a nightmare about the upcoming battle. The Urim and the ephod were not emitting any voices. Neither was the voice of the prophet active. There was nobody to answer Saul, even though he was frantically searching for help.

Similarly, we ought to live our lives in such a way that when we are gone, people going through challenging crises would wish that we were back. If we have successfully overcome serious trials and difficulties, we can pass down significant life lessons we have learned from these experiences to our children, grandchildren, friends, and acquaintances.

In your own life, there have been times you have faced a crisis, and perhaps the voice of reason, counsel, and wisdom was your father or mother or grandparent, or even some teacher or pastor. But now they are gone. Then you come face to face with a crisis, and you say something like, "I wish _____ was here right now." You wish for that because they have lived their lives in such a way that even though they are gone now, you wish that they were back. You may ask yourself, "How would they handle this?" or say, "I wish my father was here," or "The pastor would do this." But you can also live your life with such wisdom and faith that when you are gone, somebody would hope that *you* were back.

Live so that people will be shocked by the power of your memory.

In Saul's kingdom, all the lines to the psychic spiritualists were supposed to have been disconnected. This is actually Old Testament law that both Moses and Samuel advocated. Saul actually banned all contact with soothsayers and prognosticators. But apparently these people had the exact rebellious disposition that Saul showed when God told him to eliminate the Amalekites, which he did—except for the king and the best sheep.

All of the spiritualists were supposed to be gone, yet Saul was looking for a medium. One of his men told him where one was, so he disguised himself, sneaked past the Philistine army, and made his way to Endor where the witch lived. Now, this is not a glamorous witch like the one featured on the *Twilight* sagas; this is a hag. Saul begs her to hold a séance to call forth someone from the dead. But she was frightened for her life because of Saul's ban against spiritualism. He reassured her that he would protect her from being executed. When she calls up Samuel in verse 12, she reacts to his image with screams.

In verse 14 Saul falls prostrate on the floor because he is shocked by the power of the memory of Samuel. Likewise, live your life in such a way that people will be shocked by the power of your memory. That is, let people say what they want about you, but leave godly values and morals and ethics and righteousness behind you so that people will be shocked by the power of your memory.

Every family has had that kind of shocking person. It might be the matriarch or patriarch of the family. When this individual walks through the door, all "fun" stops. With family reunions, everyone wants to know when this person is coming because there are a lot of activities that are off-limits when he or she shows up. Then the family members try to get rid of this person as soon as possible so they can have their fun.

You ought to live your life in such a way that your righteousness and morals and ethics and values affect the people around you. It might not be a compliment that anything goes when you come around. That is what happens when you live out a Christianity in which you are free to say and do and be whatever you want. Instead, when you show up, certain things should be called into order.

Live so people will think of you in reverence.

In verses 14 and 20, when Samuel came, twice Saul fell on his face because he was reminded of the prophet's authority; therefore, he showed him reverence. The opposite of this is remembering people for their silliness, idiocy, or foolishness. These are living lightweights, jokers, and wild cards.

When you think of Alfred E. Neuman, you remember that he is the fictional cover boy of *MAD* magazine. This magazine has strange cartoons and offbeat caricatures, but overall it is just silly and does not offer anything important to your life. *MAD* magazine is just something to laugh at.

You should not live your life in such a silly, frivolous way that the only thing people remember about you is that they could laugh at you—that you were always the joker's wild and nobody took you seriously. Even if you tried to talk about God, people would just start laughing and doubting your sincerity. Yet, there comes a time in every believer's life when he needs to have a little weight in his conversation and lifestyle.

You ought not to be the same today as you were last year. There ought to be a factor in your lifestyle that indicates you are godlier than you used to be. It is called "character." You ought to have character that is continually being redeveloped. When people look at you, they ought to say, "There is a life worth living."

The people whom you often refer to are not the ones who are silly. Acting stupid just does not go very far. The teacher whom you remember the most, for example, was the one who made you work and study. You may have not liked him or her at the time, but you still remember that person's powerful impact on your life.

Daniel Marsh, the famed Yale scholar, used beautiful poetic language when preaching about one of the night scenes in the Bible as it relates to this very passage. Nowadays, however, people reject meaningful poetic rhetoric for impromptu staccato wording. But something would happen if they would just slow down and immerse themselves in the rich material of literary works. That is why people do not take the time to study the Bible—because they cannot speed-read it.

Live so that people will remember your words of wisdom.

In verse 15, Samuel has been called from the grave by the witch. He says, "Why have you disturbed me by bringing me up?" In other words, Samuel is rebuking Saul because he had served him as his prophet and counselor, but Saul had refused to heed his words. Instead, the arrogant king always did the exact opposite. Samuel is basically saying, "You did not listen to me to me while I was alive. Why are you disturbing me now when I am dead?"

Samuel then delivers a word of wisdom to Saul, but it is not a new revelation. He is actually repeating the same message he gave to Saul while he was alive. But now he adds a few words to it. In verses 16 and 17, Samuel says, "He [God] has turned away from you and become your enemy. The Lord has done what He has predicted through me. The Lord has torn the kingdom from you." (The last time he told Saul these words, he just added the phrase, " . . . and given it to your neighbor." This time, he names the neighbor—David.) Samuel is essentially saying, "The Lord is giving the kingdom to David because you did not know how to appreciate what He has given to you." In verse 19, Samuel adds that Saul will join him in the afterlife the next day.

Many times modern-day preachers have become buffoons in the eyes of the world by the things they have done and said. They have reduced the preaching of God's Word to a profit-making enterprise. But fortunately, God still has some Samuels left. And when God speaks through them, you had better listen to what He has to say. You do not have to like them, but if they are delivering the message God has for you, you must put your dislike aside and listen to what He has to say through them.

In the past, Saul never heeded the word of God delivered through Samuel. Now, when he desperately needs to hear from God, the Lord refuses to answer him. In the same way, you should not live your life like those who think that God should answer them every time they call, no matter how sinful their lifestyles are. God is not a genie in a bottle. Nor is He a spare tire in the trunk of your life that you can just pull out and put on when your circumstances go flat—just so you can roll to the gas station, fix your life, and then reshelve Him. That is not how God works. And if you keep rejecting what God says, there will come a time when you will need Him and He will not answer.

Today many pastors have said that you can live any way you want to. They do not want to mention the word "sin" because they fear it would offend the religious sensibilities of people and result in their attendance at other churches. But the problem people have is not psychological or emotional; they do indeed have a sin problem. No psychiatrist can deal with their sin. Instead, they need a Savior who can cleanse them of their sins.

Saul went to the witch's cave to call Samuel up from the grave. Samuel came back on request, and the message that he gave Saul was bad news. After he delivered the word of God to him, he went back to where he came from.

Yet there is another one who came up from the grave, but no witch called Him up. He arose from the dead on His own authority and stood up on His own power. Then He delivered good news, not bad, to His disciples: "I will be with you always, even unto the end of the ages. I will never leave you nor forsake you." But then He did not go back to the grave; instead, He went back to the Father. He sent us the Holy Spirit to remind us that from now on, we have someone who speaks to us beyond the grave.

When Samuel got up, he reminded Saul of defeat; but when Jesus got up, He reminded us that we live in victory. That is, we can overcome every burden or circumstance, every crisis, every challenge, every difficulty—not by our power, but by the power of God Himself. ✤

CHAPTER NINE

Looking Back at Samuel

We have looked at Samuel's life in episodes. We experience life that way ourselves. We cannot assess life as a whole until we look back and place everything we can into perspective. In the midst of the moment we are never able to give appropriate weight to that particular moment. Closer to the end of that succession of moments called "life," we may do better when looking in retrospect. We have thought through the episodes of Samuel's life together. Now we can look back, zoom out, and find some perspective.

The fruit that falls close to the tree

The affecting story of Hannah sets a trajectory for the life of Samuel. She lived in devotion to God, but also in disappointment due to the circumstances of her life. In a culture that considered barrenness a curse from God, she seemed to be a walking contradiction—devout but devoid. Yet just as is the case in many disappointments, God had a larger purpose in mind. Could she ever have imagined that 3,000 years later you would be reading the story of this Israelite woman who so wanted a baby? Similarly, your own life story may be larger than you think.

She did what anybody should do when life delivers a disappointment: She took it to God at the house of the Lord. She prayed intensely with a sense of desperation. She did not care what anyone thought about her passionate prayer. She was even faced with questions from the man of God, Eli, about the intensity of her petition to Him. (How often do we not get our deliverance because we are more interested in our dignity? We want to appear smug, above it all, aloof and not really the needy, desperate persons we are before God.) Hannah did not care how anyone felt about her intensity. She needed the intervention of God and had no self-consciousness whatsoever about asking God for His answer.

We get so intense about that which does not matter. We line up all night to get a ticket to the game, run over one another to get an autograph, wait outside the big-box store on Black Friday, and live or die with the adventures of our favorite team. We spend our days in intensity for that which vanishes. Do you think God might give you the grace to be passionate about the ultimate thing? More recently, evangelical Christians are discovering the grace of retreating to unexpected places where they passionately seek God. Some, for example, go into the desert, where absolute silence dominates, to focus totally on the quest for the presence of God. You may find the necessity to get away from noise, hurry, and crowds to be alone with God.

At first Eli mocked Hannah for the way she was praying. Then his mockery turned into blessing when he promised her an answer to prayer. Likewise, the opinion of others about your walk with God will vary from mockery to respect, from dismissiveness to dignity. You must not live your life before God with an eye toward the reaction of others. They cannot enter the sanctuary of your soul. They cannot discern the detours of your journey that lead to your destiny. Just as did Hannah, you will be surprised at the ways God vindicates you with others. Those who laugh at you one day may laud you the next. Their reactions are in His hands.

The great Spurgeon of London was the object of the most vicious ridicule in his young ministry. By the time he died at 56, however, the nation loved him and millions praised him. Indeed, God does turn things around.

Hannah set the agenda for Samuel's life by keeping her vow to God. The Lord gave her the baby Samuel, and she gave him back to the Lord.

Dr. James Earl Massey wished to be a concert pianist, but God called him to the ministry. So, he gave the keyboard back to God. The Lord let him keep that and added more than he could ever have imagined.

You will never go wrong when you give back to God what He gave to you. Your gifts and graces will be refined, fulfilled, and enriched when you place them back into the hands of God. Hannah gave Samuel back to God, and now both of them belong to the ages. A million girls bear the name "Hannah." Millions of boys carry the name "Samuel." No one today could have imagined that at that remote shrine, God was doing something for the ages.

This is God calling.

How often do you look at your caller ID? I use it to sift out telephone spam—unwanted and intrusive robo-calls from irritating solicitors. What if you could have a spiritual caller ID? Would it not be used at any moment to recognize the call of God?

Surely one of the most beloved Sunday school stories from childhood is the call of God to little Samuel. There, in a quiet and remote place, the God of the universe spoke to a little child, and that word determined his destiny.

The basis of all our faith rests on the reality that God exists and speaks to us. He does not just speak in a general word, but He also addresses each one of us by name and arrests us with the personal word. Now, that personal word never contradicts His written Word; nonetheless, it *is* personal. Just as the risen Lord Jesus Christ stood outside the garden tomb, calling the name, "Mary," and the world turned on its spiritual axis at that moment, He still calls you by name. God never sends out mail to "Resident." His is always a personal address if you would just listen.

Dr. Rebekah Naylor is now in her 60s. She recently retired as a teacher of surgery at the University of Texas Southwest Medical School in Dallas. Before that she spent decades building a hospital and nursing school in Bangalore, the garden spot of southern India. She was a surgeon, chaplain, administrator, and missionary hero. For many of us her name will belong in missionary history alongside heroes such as Lott Carey and Lottie Moon. When did all of that begin? Her father, Robert E. Naylor, while pastoring First Baptist Church, Columbia, South Carolina, gave an appeal one Sunday. Little Rebekah walked down the aisle at eight years of age and professed her call from God to be a missionary surgeon. It is likely that some people encouraged her, blessed her, and left church that morning saying, "She will get over that." Fortunately, she did not. Instead, she gave her life to Jesus and her mission.

Let us never doubt that Jesus speaks to little children. Every survey conducted by evangelical seminaries demonstrates conclusively that the large majority of those who have given their lives to Christian ministry heard Jesus speak to them as little children. Do not discount His personal word to little ones. They hear more clearly, love more purely, and follow more quickly. If you have children, encourage them to listen for God's voice, tell them stories about Him, pray with them, and take them seriously when they say He spoke to them.

Nor should we lose the lesson that it takes others to interpret the call of God to us. Eli patiently reviewed the call of God to Samuel. He helped the little one weigh it, interpret it, and yield to it. God does speak to us personally, but we may not best interpret that call individually. Part of the role of the family of God is to help us listen to that call, validate it, lean into it, and walk towards it. The God who speaks does so to individuals, but that voice also echoes within the community of believers. Some silliness that has been attributed to God might have been avoided had the listener taken the supposed word from God to sincere senior saints in the community. Eli stands for all time as a reminder that we hear the call of God and understand it best in a community echoing that call. The subjectivity of the inward call of God requires the objectivity of those who help us hear it.

The word that God spoke to Samuel kept on speaking to him throughout his long and varied life. One of the comforts in the life of faith is that the God who spoke to you will keep on speaking. Sometimes believers do go through what the mystics call "the dark night of the soul." In dry periods like that, the voice of God softens or disappears. In such times the believer is comforted by the written Word of God and lives with faith that the personal word of address will return. You can be confident that the Lord who spoke to you will speak again. You will know it is His voice because it validates itself.

For young Samuel at Shiloh, this experience began a lifetime of hearing God. In his position as a man in between the times, his listening to the voice of God was critical not only for him, but for the nation. Indeed, his attentive soul was part of the entire story of salvation history. Had he anointed any son of Jesse other than David, the very ancestry of Jesus would have been changed. This reminds us that listening to God is never a private occupation. Fathers listen for the sake of their families, and when they do not listen, it may greatly affect them for a lifetime. Mothers listen on behalf of their children. Pastors listen to God for vision and direction for their churches. Presidents hear God so they can better lead their nations. Your acuteness of hearing a word from God is never merely subjective and personal. We are all bound together in life, and how we hear from God directs or diverts the paths of others.

In fact, Samuel's hearing of the word from God touches this very moment. As I am depressing the keys of this keyboard, tiny electrical impulses are digitally recording the fact that 3,000 years ago this man named Samuel heard the word of God. The fact that you are reading this demonstrates the impact of one man, who, at the right time and place, heard God speak and responded.

May those who come behind us find us faithful in the way we hear.

Be careful when you get what you want.

Alton Parker, Charles Hughes, James Cox—I'll bet those names do not ring a bell. They all lost presidential elections in the 20th century. As contested as political elections are today, you might think everyone would remember losers as well as winners. Yet that has not usually been the case. Those who thought they should be President but were not elected tend to disappear from the American consciousness. I wonder how many of them second guessed the direction of their pursuit and their destiny.

At some point in your life, you'll come to a split in the road. You must take one route and not another. You know your choice will change your destiny, but you never know how much until you take that road. Surely the Israelites had some sense of anticipation regarding their irreversible destiny when they clamored for a king against the will of God and the intuition of Samuel. They saw the surrounding nations and empires with kings, so they desired similarity rather than uniqueness. Indeed, that choice sealed their destiny.

Life's most significant moments seldom come with a big neon sign in front of them and a voice out of heaven saying, "This is a big moment." Most of the biggest moments in our lives did not appear that big when we made those particular choices.

Because of their insistent demand for a king, the Israelites endured Saul, enjoyed David, tolerated Solomon, and then watched a civil war that divided them into two kingdoms never to be united again. All of the rebellions, wars, intrigue, exiles, dispersions, and calamities that followed flowed from their demand for a king so they could be like the other nations.

You may be familiar with the story of King Midas. He wished that everything he touched turn to gold, but then he touched his own daughter. Someone has suggested that there is a reverse Midas touch: everything you touch of value turns to something of no value. You reverse the desirable to the undesirable. In a way, that became the decision of the Israelite people when they demanded a king. God had given them a legacy of His leadership, delivery, intervention, and protection, yet they snubbed all that and wished to exchange a theocracy (the rule of God) for a mere monarchy (the rule of one man).

Do you ever watch the PBS phenomenon, "The Antique Roadshow"? Sometimes people bring in for an appraisal what they think is junk, only to find out they have a treasure. On the other hand, some people bring in what they think are treasures, only to be surprised that they have nothing of worth. The show thrives on surprises. People often do not know if they have a treasure or a piece of junk.

In the same way, Israel could have taken their desire for a king to God for His appraisal had they wished to know how to avoid the calamities at the end of the road they chose. The lesson you can take away from this story is that it is best to make the choice God wishes you to make.

One of the strangest mysteries of human freedom versus divine sovereignty is the willingness of God to let us have what we want, even when He clearly does not will that for us. The famed Oxford scholar C.S. Lewis once noted that the best thing a human can say to God is, "Thy will be done," and the worst thing God can say to a human is, "Thy will be done." There is something ominous when God simply lets us go, takes His restraining hand away, and lets us have what we want to have.

Consider the image of a boat tied to a tree a mile

upstream from a dangerous waterfall. A crazy person in the boat might rage and rant, "Someone untie the boat right now!" Finally, someone unties the boat. That nameless looser of the knot did not push the boat over the waterfall. The one who unties the rope merely turns the boat and the man in it over to the consequences of such a request.

In the same way, you can pester God to cut the rope to get what you want. The story of Israel's clamor for a king demonstrates that sometimes in the mysterious balance between your freedom and His sovereignty, He does cut the rope. Then things take their course.

A young woman begs God to give her a young man whom she wants to marry. Parents, friends, neighbors, perhaps even those closest to the young man, urge her not to pursue the union. Yet she does, and the inevitable happens. This story could be repeated about every sin of humanity: "Give me . . . Let me . . . I want it . . . Don't hold me back . . . It is my moment," and so on. It is an unfathomable mystery when God lets go of the rope and the river of destiny carries us to what awaits downstream.

I want to tell God, "Hold the rope" because I realize He knows best. I thank God that He has not let me have what I thought I have wanted. I thank God that He has held the rope—even when I wanted to cut it. We would all do well to pray to the merciful God, "Hold the rope."

Playing chess on three levels

Do you remember the chess set on the original "Star Trek" television series? Captain Kirk and Mr. Spock played chess on a board that was not only horizontal, but also vertical. You can still find Star Trek chessboards on the Internet. Chess is challenging enough to me when it is played on one level. To play chess both back and forth *and* up and down is a complex challenge beyond most humans' capacity.

When it comes to God's ability to operate at several levels, there is no question about it: He always operates on more levels than we could ever grasp. He is not locked into doing one thing at a time, one moment at a time. It takes all of the attention and focus that most of us can muster just to do one thing at a time effectively. In contrast God is able to relate to billions of people at once, thereby relating what He is doing in the life of one of us to all of the rest of us in such a way that we can never detect all that He is doing.

We find that to be true in 1 Samuel 9 and 10. Saul thinks he is only chasing after his father's runaway donkeys, when he has actually been set on a path to meet Samuel and be named king of Israel. Samuel thinks he is going to a rural village, Zuph, to hold a worship service. The moment at hand holds more for both of them than either of them could ever imagine.

Who can ever know what is wrapped up in one moment of time? Can you not recall an event in your life that was filled with destiny, yet you had no idea of the significance of that particular moment at the time? You may remember an appointment, a casual meeting with an old friend, an incidental encounter with someone seated next to you on an airplane or train, a seat assignment of a person next to you in an English class, or an introduction to a total stranger . . . and that moment held a significance for the rest of your life. We should realize that any moment, no matter how insignificant it appears at the time, is filled with such possibilities.

This means there are no insignificant places. Wherever you find yourself at this very moment may be the place where God is acting to change everything. We tend to associate great moments with august places: a cathedral, a beautiful park, a college chapel, a famous shrine, or some other obviously significant venue. We would do better to understand that God may be at work at the dry cleaner's counter, the grocery store, the quick stop market, the street corner, or the barbershop. You cannot identify where God may be waiting to change everything.

This also suggests there are no unlikely times for God to work. Some think He prefers to do His business on Sunday mornings between 8:00 a.m. and noon. But God may just as well be working at 4:00 a.m. when a barking dog awakens you and you review your life while trying to go to sleep. God may be working when the club closes at 2 a.m. and you head home, disappointed that life has brought you no significant relationships as you look squarely at the emptiness of your own heart. God may be working at noon on your lunch hour when a bird singing in a downtown tree reminds you of a joy and freedom you wish you had. When Saul arrived at Zuph broke and disappointed, he did not know that in that very moment the remainder of his life rested.

At the same time, you may want to consider the concept that there are no unimportant people you encounter. We tend to think that famous, popular, charming, or powerful people are the very ones who could change everything for us. Saul and his unnamed servant met some girls coming down a hill who told them Samuel was in town. That incognito group of young women held one of the keys to Saul's destiny. Without them, the chain of what God was doing would have been broken.

On every bottle of Tabasco® sauce you will find the name of the family who still owns the iconic American brand—McIlhenny. After the Civil War the first McIlhenny returned to his wife's home on Avery Island, Louisiana. He was a broke banker with worthless bank notes. A mysterious man in New Orleans on the street gave him a handful of pepper seeds that he said were from Tabasco, Mexico. Out of curiosity McIlhenny planted the seeds. That seemingly insignificant event marked the origin of one of the most famous brands in the world.

At any moment you may meet someone who could hand you the seeds to your own future. Be aware that an encounter you did not expect could produce a harvest you cannot believe. Never forget to consider each encounter with every person a moment of significance. This piece of advice also suggests how you should treat people in each encounter. If any meeting with a child of God may be fraught with significance, you must be very careful how you relate to the next person you meet. That person may be the very angel of God sent to bless you and open your future. On the other hand, you may unwittingly be the messenger of God to that person.

You will also find that the more sensitive you are to significant moments, more of them will happen to you. If you sleepwalk through life, never aware that any moment could be a moment of change, you will miss out on some significant moments. On the other hand, if you greet each day on tiptoe with expectancy, you will have more significant moments than you would otherwise. Don't miss your moment.

In 1 Samuel 10 Saul found that God would give him significant encouragement along the way—solid confirmations that he was walking the way God intended. God made prearrangements for Saul to meet persons who assured him with provisions and spiritual encouragement. Similarly, when you are walking toward your destiny, you will find that God often places in your pathway just the very persons who encourage you at the moment you most need it. If you will review your own walk with God, you will remember such people. It was almost as if they had been posted where they were to wait for that very moment. An e-mail, a letter, a phone call, or a casual conversation lit the way for the rest of that period in your life. Indeed, you can trust God to send just the right people at the right place and time to inspire you in your life journey.

A view from the back of the hearse

Although it is a sober thought, we should be reminded that one day they will put what is mortal about us in a box, put that box in the back of a hearse, and take us to the cemetery. What if that were you, and you could look out the back of the hearse at those in the procession? What would they be saying about you on their way to bury you in the ground? That statement may seem silly, stark, or surprising, but it is a reality about life. You will leave a legacy. When the folks are following that hearse to the cemetery, what will they be saying about you?

Samuel demonstrated a concern about his legacy in one of his last speeches to the nation. He wanted to leave with a clear conscience, a clean slate, an unimpeachable legacy. He inventoried his own conscience and weighed his own past actions. He offered to make everything right with anyone he had wronged. He discussed this right down to the particulars: if he had taken anyone's ox, he wanted to give an ox back! He wanted to do what he could do to make things right before he left the planet.

Dr. Fred Craddock tells of sitting in a plane by a young woman who was obviously upset. After he told her that he was a minister, she mentioned that she had just attended her father's funeral. Then she unburdened herself to him with the rest of the story. She had received an urgent call from the hospital that her father was dying. During the time it took for her to fly across the country in order to see him alive, however, he died. She was one hour late. Ten years ago, they had parted in anger on the telephone and had not spoken since. They never made it right. She had to look into the frozen features of a deceased father with whom she had not been reconciled. How did the back of the hearse look to her? What if he could have sat up and looked out of the back of the hearse at the family car? How would he have felt?

Reconciliation and restitution both have a time limit. On milk cartons they print expiration dates: the milk must be either sold or drank by that date. Life itself, however, does not come marked with clear expiration dates. We do not know and cannot tell when its opportunities expire. It would be interesting if some blazing letters in the sky would write out, "Expiration date on making things right with your sister will be TOMORROW." Yet, such does not happen. Life slips by. Days vanish. Time expires.

Samuel also reminds us that what he said had come to pass. His word was true. His promises were reliable. As hard as it seems to believe, in Texas until recently, multiple-million dollar deals were done in the oil patch and on the cattle trail with a handshake. The best thing you could say about a man was, "His word is his bond." The worst thing you could say was, "He broke his promise." Businesses were built and fortunes made on the reliability of a person's word. Unfortunately, that world is now gone. Today when you close on a house at the mortgage company, you even have to sign a ridiculous paper that simply says you are who you are! So devious have people become that you have to affirm that you are who you are. What a great grace to leave the legacy that you stood by your word. If you could sit up and look out of the back of the hearse, would the folks affected by your promises say, "He kept his word," or, "What she said, she did"?

The hard art of walking away

You must sympathize with Samuel when it comes to his reluctance to abandon Saul. He had met Saul when the king was just a youth. He had whispered to him that he would be king. He had anointed him. He had advised him. Samuel had a deep personal stake in Saul. Yet the time came when God told Samuel to walk away. Samuel was not commanded to walk away because Samuel had no affection for Saul. Instead, Samuel was ordered to walk away because Saul had become toxic to the very plan of God for Israel.

Surely one your hardest decisions will be to walk away from those whose very presence is toxic to God's will for your life and God's work in your world. A hard but certain fact belongs to some moments in your life journey. You have to leave someone behind in God's hands because they endanger the attainment of the will of God in your life. Be very careful not to misunderstand what I am saying: Some covenants in life are never meant to be broken. You are not supposed to walk out on a marriage if your spouse has not committed adultery or abused you. You must not quit being a parent to the child you have brought into the world. Those relationships are not negotiable. God never told anyone to leave a marriage partner except for adultery or abuse, or to abandon a child. So, do not misunderstand me here.

Outside of those sacred parameters, however, God will tell you to end some relationships. Some people you know are toxic to your spiritual well-being. You are positive, full of faith, and energized by prayer, but then you find yourself around a certain somebody who pushes every negative button in you. Your positive faith turns into negative doubt. Your energized prayer turns into listless prayerlessness. And this does not just happen once; it happens every time you are in their presence. Another acquaintance drags you down into destructive habits that you thought you had left behind forever. Still another mocks your faith and demeans your church. These certain people do not do what they do once, but rather as the habitual direction of their lives and the dominant theme of their days. These individuals do not occasionally call out your worst, but they do it constantly when you are in their presence. When Jesus seems far away, the Holy Spirit appears to be on a vacation, and the Father above does not smile, you know it is time to go. You have to leave.

In the horror movies, do you recall that dramatic way living persons could send Dracula back to the place from which he came? They drove a silver spike through his heart. It had to be decisive, quick, without hesitation, and final. Now, do not go around driving stakes into the heart of people, or you will go where Dracula went! Yet metaphorically and figuratively, you sometimes have to be just that decisive with a relationship that poisons your spiritual life and lethally contaminates your faith. You must deal with it all at once.

A little boy owned a new dog, an English bulldog. This breed has to have its tail shortened—a practice called docking. But the little boy did not want the vet to cut the dog's tail off. One afternoon his mother inside the house heard the dog yelping with unearthly screams. Then there was quiet, followed by another bout of awful howling. Then there was quiet again. This happened six times. The mother went out and saw six one-inch pieces of the dog's tail. She was horrified. The little boy had a pair of her sewing scissors.

"What in God's name have you done?" the mother cried.

The little boy replied, "I thought it would hurt less if I cut it off one inch at a time."

At the expense of the dog that endured such terrible pain, the child was sadly mistaken.

Regarding bad relationships, you must cut them off all at once, and they will end up hurting less. But if you linger around a poisonous person, tarry beside a toxic situation, and cut it off one inch at a time, the final severing of the relationship will only take longer and cause more pain. Just as ripping a bandage quickly off a wound hurts less, ending toxic relationships quickly will also hurt less in the long run. That is what God told Samuel, and that is what He is telling you. Sometimes you must leave people and situations in the hands of God and go forward into God's future for you.

At the same time, God always has the next person for His work and kingdom in place. That certain individual may be the most unlikely person to accomplish His word, but God knows who it is. David was the eighth son of Jesse and was not even considered a candidate to be anointed as king. Nevertheless, Samuel had to look beyond the external to the internal—to the very heart of David.

Are you able to discern the hearts of people? To some degree we are all always a puzzle, a walking contradiction. Yet God does expect you to use the gift of discernment, the sensitive guidance of the Holy Spirit, as you encounter different people and situations.

Have you ever spent a week in the pure mountain air at the timberline? When you come back to the city, you are more sensitive to every fragrance. In the same way, when you dwell with the Holy Spirit, you become sensitive to the spiritual atmosphere. You do not judge, but you do discern. You are not unkind, but you are graciously firm. Some situations and people do not belong in your life, so you graciously excuse yourself. At other times you sense the new thing that God wishes you to do, and eagerly accept the new person whom He sends into your life.

Be aware that such situations always reflect the truth of the Scriptures. God does not contradict His holy Word. If you think you have Mr. Right but he never prays, never goes to church, and has left a trail of broken relationships in his wake, he is not even Mr. Almost Right. The best remedy for you is a good pair of sneakers. Run! God will give you discernment. When you have it, act.

Perhaps the greatest lesson in the life of Samuel is the memorable phrase, "Man looks at the outward appearance, but God looks at the heart." How many relationships have been based on the opposite of that? Here is Miss Hottie, and you just know that life would be a perpetual blessing if you could just wake up every morning looking at her. Here is Mr. Wonderful, who looks like a combination of George Clooney and Denzel Washington. You just know that your life would be heaven on earth if you could just be with him. Then you get her or him. You find out that you should have had a brain transplant to have made such a choice. This is just one example of looking at the outward appearance, an example for which many a sad man or woman could give convincing testimony. You need to develop your senses to assess the heart of a person, especially a potential marriage partner with whom you will spend your entire life.

Where do you turn when you hit bottom?

Surely 1 Samuel 28 is one of the most bizarre passages in all of the Holy Scriptures. Rejected by God, thrown for a loss about what to do next, and left all alone, a desperate Saul goes to a witch to call Samuel back from the dead for one more counseling session! You should not miss the reality that Samuel *did* come back. Nowhere does the Bible deny the possibility of demonic witchcraft trafficking with the underworld. There is a demonic, dark, and deathly world with which you do not want to be acquainted. Indeed, it has a stark reality.

A friend of mine once heard Nicky Cruz, a character from David Wilkerson's book *The Cross and the Switchblade,* in person describe New York City gang members who made a pact with the Devil. They so sold themselves to the Evil One that they no longer had to crack locks; they just pointed at them and they opened.

That is a place you do not want to go. The Bible never denies the power of the world of darkness. It *does* warn us not to go there.

Where do you turn when you are out of options? Do you go to the self-help section of the bookstore, the Ouija board, the Tarot cards, a fortune cookie, or a palm reader? We could all list the ridiculous and sometimes dangerous places to which we turn in order to find out what to do next when we are at our wit's end. We seem to turn anywhere other than the clear promise of the Word of God: "If any of you lacks wisdom, let him ask God, who gives to all liberally and without reproach, and it will be given to him" (James 1:5). We have a categorical promise from God for wisdom itself—if we just ask Him in faith. God delights to give wisdom in our worst extremities.

Saul did not get the word he wanted when Samuel came back from the dead. Instead, he received a word that only gave him stark terror about his own future. I wonder what would have happened if Saul had turned to the living God, the source of all wisdom, and pleaded with Him for mercy and direction? What if he had cast himself on the grace of God, as David did in Psalm 51? We can never know what would have happened, but it would have been a better course than what Saul took.

In the final analysis, the lesson to take away from this

story and all of the stories about Samuel is not that we are to *be like* Samuel or *unlike* Saul. Biblical characters often belong to the history of world salvation; their circumstances, challenges, and actions belong to the biblical story of the history of redemption. That is, their stories are not included in the Bible as mere individual object lessons. They have a bigger purpose than just giving you a pattern for living.

The purpose for looking at Samuel and Saul is to actually look through them and beyond them at the living God. Samuel and Saul are both still very much alive in an eternal world. Jesus Himself said, "God is not the God of the dead but of the living" (Matthew 22:32). If they could speak directly to you from the life beyond, they would not tell you to be like them or unlike them. They would point you to Him, the living God, as the One to whom you turn for all things.

The ultimate takeaway from all biographical preaching points you to God and God alone. For Christians He is seen in the face of Jesus Christ. You cannot know more about God than what Jesus tells you, and He is all that you need. In the last analysis, you do not need Samuel for anything more than to point you toward God and His revelation in Christ: "But of Him you are in Christ Jesus, who became for us wisdom from God—and righteousness and sanctification and redemption" (1 Corinthians

1:30). Short of Jesus Christ, the worth of any Bible character only counts when pointing us to God, who finally revealed Himself in Jesus.

- Did Hannah follow through on the will of God? Even more so did Jesus.
- Did little Samuel hear the voice of the Father? Jesus heard it all the more perfectly.
- Did Samuel and Israel struggle with the perfect will of God for a king? Jesus struggled with the will of God in Gethsemane and chose rightly, while Israel chose wrongly.
- Did Samuel experience divine timing in his walk with God? Jesus lived with that timing perfectly, knowing when and where His hour had come.
- Could Samuel look back on a life of integrity? Jesus could look back on an eternity of oneness with the Father, during which He never disobeyed Him.
- Did Samuel have to walk away from Saul after making that hard choice? Jesus walked away from the Tempter in the wilderness, making the hard choice of the cross.
- Did Samuel come back from the life beyond only to return to the grave? Jesus came forth from the open, empty tomb, never to return again to the land of the dead, but to take you from the land of the dead to the land of the living. ❖

NOTES

NOTES

NOTES